FORGOTTEN
TOWNS
of
SOUTHERN
NEW JERSEY

FORGOTTEN
TOWNS
of
SOUTHERN
NEW JERSEY

by Henry Charlton Beck

RUTGERS UNIVERSITY PRESS
New Brunswick   *London*

Fourteenth printing, 1994

Manufactured in the United States of America

Library of Congress Cataloging in Publication Data

Beck, Henry Charlton, 1902–1965.
  Forgotten towns of southern New Jersey.

  1. City and town life—New Jersey.   2. New Jersey—
History, Local.   3. New Jersey—Social life and customs.
I. Title.
F134.B44   1983   974.9'9   83-9695
ISBN 0-8135-1016-3 (pbk.)
British Cataloging-in-Publication Information Available.

To
MY WIFE
who first believed in it,
MY MOTHER
who inspired the patience to wait for it,
and
MY FATHER
whose love of the outdoors binds all of us together forever,
this book is lovingly dedicated.

FOREWORD TO 1961 PRINTING

When *Forgotten Towns of Southern New Jersey* was published by E. P. Dutton and Company, of New York, in 1936, it was my hope to prepare another book on south Jersey, two on the midlands, and two on the upper end of the state. At least this was in my mind; and Merton S. Yewdale and Louise Townsend Nicholl, who were editors at Dutton's in those days, gave every encouragement to the project.

Admittedly I had little to recommend me apart from a young reporter's enthusiasm and three or four detective novels, but this first book and its successors, *More Forgotten Towns* and *Fare to Midlands*, which appeared in 1937 and 1939, fared comparatively well. I think this may have been because few people until then had considered that there could possibly be ghost towns in New Jersey. Or perhaps it was because of what the editors were kind enough to define as a combination of nostalgia, freshness of approach, and a certain naïveté of discovery on the part of the chronicler.

Then came times of war, and when my schedule was resumed, I had become convinced that the story of the unsung Mullica River must be told—in the recollections and language of those who still lived in their ancestors' homes along its banks. So, in 1945, *Jersey Genesis* was born.

The manuscript of this book was rejected by a number of publishers, and finally, feeling that the story of the Mullica belonged to the state university, as well as to New Jersey itself, I sent it along to my old friend, Wallace S. Moreland, then assistant to the president of Rutgers University. The life of *Jersey Genesis* was meteoric, and it heartens me to know that it, too, may soon be reprinted. My most recent book, *The Roads of Home*, which tells the story of more of my journeyings, all over the state, was published in 1956 and is now in its third printing.

I must tell you that *Forgotten Towns of Southern New Jersey* is composed, for the most part, of sketches that were published weekly in the *Courier-Post* newspapers of Camden, New Jersey, of which I subsequently became State Editor. The sketches never were meant to be read as straight or even neat history, even in revised form. They were gleaned, in factual reporting, from the people and places whose stories I wanted to tell—and their basic validity is proved, I should think, by the loving confidence these people and places have continued to express. In all my books, as well as in the series of articles that I have been writing for the Newark *Star-Ledger* for over fifteen years, my concern has been with folklore rather than history as such. Thus, I have taken the best I could find and kept an open mind for change or variant. What you will find in this book is the story of what I

5

actually found or saw and what was told to me by Jersey people, some twenty-five years ago.

Ong's Hat still has its identifying tree, but no Eli Freed. Batsto, ignored for so long, has become a state preserve, its curators intent on learning as much as they can about this important industrial center of Revolutionary times. Speedwell is now a turn in an improved road, with its slag pile all but obliterated. Some villages and hamlets of the past have been swallowed up by newcomers or erased by military establishments, or else they have simply faded away. About them all, by this time, there can be told new stories, different stories; but none would have emerged without the telling of the first. Today there are four different legends of how Ong's Hat, or Ong's Hut, got its name, and I have a notion that I may hear of at least one more.

At first I was dismayed at the idea of a reissue of *Forgotten Towns* because I knew that the people and places as I wrote of them in the early thirties could never be discovered that way again—I had midnight dreams of drivers all but wrecking their cars to find some thing or someone no longer there, of other travelers baffled and frustrated by new roads and people where once there were but swamps and sand trails and cedar water and silence. At last, persuaded more than ever that the people of New Jersey should become more keenly aware of *all* their heritage, not just around their homes but all over the state—in the mountains, in the flatlands, on the seacoast, and in the forest fastnesses—I have consented to this reissue. Dealers in old books may regret the appearance of this new printing, but the people who love New Jersey, for what it was, what it is, and what it will be, perhaps will not be disappointed. At least this is my hope.

HENRY CHARLTON BECK

Lawrenceville, New Jersey
June, 1961

FOREWORD

THE writing and revision of the stories which appear in this book represent the accurate chronicle of part of a most unusual and fascinating adventure. It began when the foreman of a newspaper composing-room, always ready with ideas for making busy people busier, proposed that an honest effort should be made to locate the town still indicated on maps of New Jersey by the mysterious name of Ong's Hat. It has gone on beyond Southern New Jersey and now, slowed down by the complexities of depression and recovery, as reflected in newspapers generally, it has paused for reflection and second wind.

Although Ong's Hat had been a name for the best part of a century, no one had ever taken it seriously, apparently. Once a managing editor had written some amusing stuff about it in his column on the editorial page. But the exactness of its location, just who lived in its domain and who were its ruling officials, if any, had remained unknown.

In consequence we set out next day—a State Editor and a photographer—in a car of uncertain functioning, determined to run Ong's Hat, and all relating to it, definitely to earth. The result of that first quest is the first sketch in this book. The history and modern status of Ong's Hat, however, failed to appease either the inquisitors' or the popular appetite, and the search for Forgotten Towns, thus informally begun, has become a "business" that is still going on.

A few of the stories which appeared in several series in

the now defunct *Sunday Courier-Post*, the *Evening Courier* and the *Morning Post* of Camden, New Jersey, have been omitted because in comparison with the others selected here, they seemed somewhat drab of content. All of them, however, have brought a continued response from those who have read them, surprising even the author. Some letters he has received have found fault with unimportant detail but the majority have expressed keen interest and helpful appreciation of the quest. In this regard I would like to say that every effort has been made to make these narratives accurate and that at no time have they been colored by what is sometimes jocularly referred to as a newspaper imagination. A few critics, I am afraid, have based their contentions on the fact that the dull grist of history has been coated with a much more readable fancy; that, I contend, is something of an accomplishment.

As these stories were written, many towns, too tiny and uncertain for placement on present-day maps, have been found to be villages of importance long before the first flares of the Revolution. Others which have vanished entirely were called to mind by those who lived near their sites, remembering the strange fireside tales of their forebears. Still other hamlets and less, mere clusters of dwellings at forsaken crossroads, have hidden their past in brooding silence and decay. While the world outside has been growing up, this world "inside" has been growing down.

Through the sketches, each complete in itself, there winds a connecting skein of untold or little known wartime history. Through each one there runs something of the Revolution, the War of 1812, the conflict of North against South with themes of early industry, of pioneers who depended on the first bog furnaces and glass-making plants for their living—people who with the abandonment of such establishments became lost in a jungle as complete as Central Africa—for contrast.

Many stories, it will be found, concern the pine towns and their people, the "pineys" who, lonely in lack of education, have lived back in the Jersey pine woods, on hidden trails and beside dismal swamps, within walking distance of modern communities, within two hours' riding distance of Philadelphia and New York City. Many untruths have been uttered about these people. Many of the conditions which served the unscrupulous for exaggeration and fake philanthropy some years ago have been completely obliterated. But here among the ruins of forgotten towns within forty miles of Philadelphia and eighty miles of New York there still live the children and grandchildren of those to whom several wives for one man was an accepted code.

These are the descendants of first settlers, bog ore miners, lumber-cutters, glassmakers, sailors and soldiers of Washington's time, Hessians who preferred to go amok in the woods to returning home, slaves who sought strange ways to celebrate their new-found liberty. The more intelligent set up hotels along the few trails of the barren, fire-swept country, journeying to town for marriage or more formal business. The rest bothered with laws and ceremonies only when it was convenient.

One story, perhaps the most persistent in this regard, is well known. A British soldier of good parentage but with uncertain ideas of living, became enamored of a barmaid in a wayside tavern and without the trouble of a wedding they became joint proprietors of the place. There came a family of eight children all of whom were later found to have mental deficiencies or criminal inclinations. The soldier, tiring of this mode of life, went back to England, married in his rightful class and began anew. At home, a family of three normal children resulted. I use this incident, perhaps already an old chestnut in New Jersey, just as a picture before you turn the page.

This book does not concern itself with morals—here are the stories of crumbling houses, piles of ore slag, broken bits of glass, tumbledown and burnt sawmills, as revealed by a few of that diminishing group of people who know of what they are relicts. The sketches from other towns, outside the pines area, are told here by way of relief.

The task of obtaining the material for these anecdotes of unwritten history, as fetching as it has been, could not have been accomplished entirely alone. I am deeply indebted to those who have acted as guides to hidden villages, as well as to those who have swept away the cobwebs of memory or paused to encourage by letter, time and again.

The name of M. Warner Hargrove will appear many times in this book and yet I feel that mere mention with the towns we "discovered" together is not enough. In the adventure of the Lost Town Expeditions he was more than a guide, more than a man with the gift of memory and imagination. He was a devoted and often too little appreciated friend. *Requiescat in pace!*

Others who must be mentioned by name for their helpfulness are Charles Remine, of Wrightstown; the late Charles E. Crate, of Collingswood; Joseph Sickler, of Salem; J. Gearhart Crate, reporter on a morning newspaper who spent one afternoon a week wearing out his little car on brier-hedged trails, and Howard Shivers, one of several cameramen who proved our stories with fine pictures. I know only too well how loyal these men have been, when cars bogged down, when break-downs required long treks through winter snows, when only a compass led us back to civilization long after working hours.

As I have already intimated, it would be virtually impossible to cram all material now at hand, after excursions of some five years, into one book. I believe that after revision I will find as many new stories in my files and notes as appear here. However, these sketches are connected by the classifications I have made, as well as the general locality of South Jersey. On the outer rim of this area, the romance of decadent things has proven just as rich.

I hope, finally, that these stories will serve to make permanent those legends of the forgotten towns which might have been lost with those who remember passing to their reward. It is my honest belief that in all of us there still lingers something of the early explorers, a something which in some measure may be appeased in retracing these journeys we have made. New roads have brought speed and traffic but the old roads sink deeper into oblivion just the same.

H. C. B.

CONTENTS

ILLUSTRATIONS

15

Forgotten Towns

of

SOUTHERN NEW JERSEY

I

ONG'S HAT

HE said his name was Eli Freed and that he wanted to borrow money somewhere to buy a horse.

Eli was the last resident of Ong's Hat, the forgotten town that began all these adventures. For years Ong's Hat had been on the map in Burlington County, but no one had done anything except make fun of it.

Although these explorations into the hinterland of Southern New Jersey took us to many strange places, Mount Misery, Woodmansie, Double Trouble and Chicken Bone, no other vanished village quite attained to the individuality of Ong's Hat in name.

Today it remains upon the map even though there is no village. There is a clearing on a rough-tarred road, not far from Four Mile. In that clearing there used to be a dilapi-dated shed, once part of the last house. But only bits of broken brick, pieces of roofing, cast-off shoes and the long, straggly Indian grass remain to convince you now that once, long ago, there was really a town.

The way to Ong's Hat winds from the Pemberton road, back across a carpet of fallen leaves, through patches of white sand and down through deep, inky ruts.

Ong's Hat, according to the lingering natives in the pine barrens, took its name from a young flame named Ong. Once we thought it unlikely that anyone with such a name actually existed but some months ago we found a whole family of Ongs down in the neighborhood of Tuckerton.

Concerning Ong, there have been two different versions of the legend. One is that he was a dancer who captivated the admiration of the girls at Saturday night dances. At that time the village, apparently still unnamed and with no distinction at all, was a huddle of houses, a dance hall and a roadside clearing where, in the Gay Nineties, gruelling semi-pro prize fights were held.

Ong, it seems, came to the dances with great regularity. He was the chief figure inasmuch as he owned a shiny high silk hat, worn with a rakish air that placed him, for the evening at least, among the clouds. There came a night when Mr. Ong failed to give one of his partners the attention she required. The young woman snatched the hat from Ong's head and deliberately stamped upon it in the middle of the dance floor. There that story ends.

The second account seems to go on from just this point. Mr. Ong, while considerably in liquor, is said to have tossed his distinguished topper high in a tree at the center of the village. There, battered and irretrievable, it hung through the wind and rain of many months. Whichever incident is based on fact, the town from then on claimed the name: Ong's Hat.

A hundred or so years ago, we were told, the place was a center of life among the pineys. There were frequent dances and couples came for miles in buggies, carryalls and on foot, to step to the music of country fiddlers. There was no Prohibition and it was more than soda pop that enlivened the crowd. There were brawls and fisticuffs, some of them bloody enough.

One of the first bootleggers known to compel the services of law and order in Local Option days was arrested at

Ong's Hat. The arrest was not for possession and sale, of course, but for selling liquor without a license. Samuel Haines was the culprit and he was taken in charge in the midst of gay festivities one night by two burly constables.

Prize fights were the main attraction. Battlers, attracted by promises of fat purses, corn liquor and pretty, dull-eyed damsels, tackled each other for a decision which was often fought over in turn by the crowd, out there in the middle of nowhere. Older natives recall one particular fight in which a negro whipped a white man, stirring up a riot that had to burn itself out. There were no telephones, no State troopers, no snooping Dry Squads in those days.

There came a later lull in which Ong's Hat was all but forgotten. Then, as has been the case with many of the lost towns of the barrens, murder suddenly carried its name to the front pages of newspapers. That happened after a Polish wanderer and his wife moved into the clearing. Mr. and Mrs. John Chininiski found the place mostly deserted even then, except by seven residents who hung on, among the memories of better days. And not long after the Chininiskis arrived, they disappeared.

The woman vanished first, without trace or rumor. Chininiski, who at first didn't seem to worry much, dropped out of sight when people began to talk. The house in which the couple had established a home stood idle for a while, partly furnished. Then it fell apart, piece by piece. The Chininiskis never came back.

Many years ago a party of hunters, walking through the woods near Ong's Hat in deer season, came suddenly upon a human skull and skeleton. These were thought, upon police examination, to be the remains of poor Mrs. Chininiski who, they theorized, had been cruelly murdered by her husband. A bundle of mouldy clothing, nailed in a box, was found near the bones.

Ellis Parker, renowned Burlington County detective celebrated in countless murder cases, took the matter in charge. Despite the years which had passed, he trailed Chininiski to New York, but there lost the scent. To this day Chief Parker, in his stuffy office in the Mt. Holly courthouse, has the woman's skull to remind him that the mystery at Ong's Hat was not solved.

Burlington County has distorted the story now. Some people will tell you that at Ong's Hat a man and woman were murdered in cold blood by scoundrels in search of money.

Discovery of that weather-bleached skeleton seems to have frightened everybody out of town—all but Eli Freed. Eli says he moved in just as all the excitement was dying down. He was seventy-nine when we were there, a soft-spoken, wrinkled old man, amazed that anybody should take the trouble to visit him. He had cleared a twenty-acre tract with his own hands, making his home in a rough-board dwelling he and his partner, a man he called Amer, built together. Freed explained that he came to Ong's Hat from Chicago where he took a sick man from the Isle of Pines.

"This part of the country is different from Chicago," the old man said seriously when he sat down in the front room of his swept-and-garnished house. "It's different from Cuba, too. I liked Cuba but there were too many storms for me. I still own property down there—and I used to be a school teacher out in the West, up in Oregon and Washington mostly. Been a widower—let's see now, forty-two years."

"You like it here?" we asked him.

"Yes, I like it," he said. "But I have a terrible time with the deer and rabbits, especially the rabbits. That's why I've got that high fence all around the place. The deer jump right over it sometimes. But I keep two cats to chase the rabbits. I'm lucky to be able to grow my turnips, potatoes and corn the way I do. I wouldn't dare try beans: the rabbits like them too much."

We mentioned watermelons, for some crazy reason.

"Watermelons?" Eli repeated, as if he were a Californian, "why, this summer we had one that was three feet long and a foot thick. Weighed fifty pounds. It lasted me and my partner two whole months!"

Then Eli Freed disclosed that he wanted a horse.

"I need one bad," he declared. "But I haven't got the money. Do you know any good place where I could borrow the money to buy a good cart-horse?"

We have wondered, sometimes, whether Eli ever got his horse. And we always laugh in remembering that prize watermelon story. Just the same they are details of the stories that identify forgotten Ong's Hat, the vanished town of murder, of prize fights and of isolated country dances.

The gristmill at Batsto, one of the few buildings to survive the big fire of 1874, was built in 1828 by ironmaster Jesse Richards.

Lake site of the furnace at Batsto, the largest producer of bog ore pig iron, cannonballs, castings, and hollow wares in the country during the Revolution.

II

BATSTO

A CELEBRATION of Independence Day never comes without bringing a thought of Batsto, Pleasant Mills, Sweetwater and the patriots surprised at Chestnut Neck.

Today, cool in the shade of its ancient trees, removed from the bustle of the workaday world, Batsto seems to have forgotten that once it was a factor in a nation's fight for freedom. The iron works where many a cannonball was moulded is gone. The old mill wheels turn no more. The inn and store no longer look for customers.

It is more than a hundred and fifty years since the British Redcoats, aroused by Yankee pirates who crippled and captured their merchantmen, pounced on the favorite resort of the privateers at Chestnut Neck, and gloating in their success, sought further to smother the fires of Batsto.

Chestnut Neck was in those war days a place of considerable importance. A thriving business was carried on there by wagonmen who shipped goods to all points along the Delaware.

New York Harbor was blockaded. Philadelphia was in enemy hands. A new port had to be found for ships carrying provisions to Washington's ill-fed army.

Great Bay, Old Egg Harbor, was selected. Cargoes of foodstuffs and other supplies were unloaded at Chestnut Neck and then carted, by wagon, to distant points on tiring journeys up to Burlington and from there to Valley Forge.

Meanwhile Chestnut Neck had armed. Elijah Clark and Richard Wescoat who had built a fort at Fox Burrows had bought for its defense a few small cannon, for which in September, 1777, the Legislature had ordered payment of four hundred and thirty pounds.

When the British attack came, however, it was something of a surprise. A letter was revealed, dated from Chestnut Neck, October fifth, stating that the enemy had been sighted and was closing in. The letter estimated the fighting array at twenty sails. Word was sent for assistance through the unbelievable medium of a newspaper, *The Pennsylvania Packet.*

The same paper announced in its issue of October tenth that New Jersey's Governor, Livingston, had received word of the intended attack and was planning measures to offstand it. He had, it was announced, sent express riders to arouse residents along the shore and announced that General Washington had already sent Count Pulaski with his foot-and-horse legion from Pennsylvania to lend assistance. But by this time most of the "campaign" was over.

The British commander, Sir Henry Clinton, had taken a long time to be convinced that the Yankees were really doing any notable damage to the British merchant fleet. He had always been an easy-going fellow and had laughed at the reports brought him of stolen ships and pirated cargoes. But finally, he leaped into action. He demanded to know what fortifications he must expect. He was told that the Neck had been mounted with earthworks facing the river and that four companies of militia were stationed there, mostly farmers and dwellers of the bay shore.

Accounts of the actual day of the battle differ. Some

writers have placed it on a fine day in April, 1778. Others have made it a misty morning of October. It is more likely that it was in the fogs of the autumn that the British made so surprising an assault. A sloop of war convoyed two transports offshore from where eight hundred British regulars were landed. This, it is mostly agreed, was October sixth.

With the fleet outside the harbor, Capt. Patrick Ferguson ordered the men to shore in galleys. These were rowed up the Mullica to Chestnut Neck, which, as the troops put in, lay silent. Its defenders had evidently spied the ships and had estimated the number of soldiers with alarm. The baymen determined, however, on a show of resistance, no matter how small it would be.

As the Redcoats set foot on the landing there was a scattered fire from the breastworks. No account shows that there was more than a clatter of musketry and one wonders what happened to the cannon, that they were not used on the approaching ships. With the Britishers on land, presumably the range was too short. The soldiers trained by His Majesty lined up in formation and charged the fort. The patriots retreated to the woods, to which their families had retired some time earlier.

A few were killed and a few more were wounded, but the commander who, the legends say, replaced a colonel who was shot down by the first volley from the enemy, saw no point in risking further loss which an untrained and smaller group must suffer from a drilled and well-directed force. The Britishers had lost but one man, but nevertheless they retreated back to the shore. There they found the largest of the prize ships already scuttled and dismantled.

The ships were set afire along with the twelve houses

that made up the village, as soon as the usual plundering had been completed. The wharf and storehouse were stripped and leveled with the breastworks. Then the invaders rested.

But Captain Ferguson wanted to make a clean sweep. He had scotched Chestnut Neck forever. What could be better than marching inland to dismantle and put the Batsto furnace out of existence?

This would, of course, necessitate an encounter with the post at The Forks as well as the crossing of the Atsion Creek. The Batsto iron works were working at fever heat. The contract for munitions was large and the demand was great. If the British could suddenly surprise the town . . .!

Ferguson marched his men from the site of the burning village and at nightfall, camped in a clearing a few miles up the shore road.

A youth named Bake, who had taken part in the battle, and who, with the others, had retreated, took advantage of the darkness and returned to spy on the Redcoats. Running from tree to tree, through the woods that skirted the road, he followed the invading host from Chestnut Neck to where camp was made. He learned, or more likely, guessed, that a new attack would be made at dawn next day. The boy made a quick detour and finding the commander of the company at the Forks, told him of what he had seen and surmised.

No time was lost. Messengers were chosen to make rides like those of Paul Revere, through the countryside. By midnight, ninety men, woodsmen, iron workers and farmers, those who had not answered the call to the colors at the munitions plant or with the army, had gathered. Of military tactics they knew little. But most of them could shoot and were fairly good marksmen. They stationed themselves in ambush along the road, not far from the British army. There they waited.

The British soldiers made no secret of their presence. They were up before dawn with blare of bugles and the staccato of orders. Soon, in the early light of the morning, they were marching down the road toward Batsto. On they moved with even tread, certain that they would completely surprise these rebels. Then their morning reveries were interrupted by the sharp command of "Fire!" From the trees there came a volley that sent even the birds screaming for quarter.

The effect was deadly. The surprise was complete. Nearly every bullet found a man. By the time the British realized what had happened, the Yankees had reloaded. There was an immediate retreat, a retreat in confusion. Officers did not care to order their men to face odds they couldn't number. The defenders, remaining hidden, continued to fire, making no attempt to follow.

Returning to their homes, the patriots met Pulaski's legion, marching to assist the rebels, but too late to be of aid. Pulaski and his men of seven nations, many trained in martial maneuvers overseas, pressed toward the coast. There they saw the transports already in flight down the river. All but one sloop, which grounded on a bar, were soon en route to New York. It had been the clash of raw scrappers against the masters of bayonet. The untrained but dauntless pioneers had come off with the victory.

They told us the story of a British corporal, a sort of unofficial prisoner of war, who was left behind as wounded by his fellows. He used to sing in a tavern near Batsto, when his voice and poetic instincts were sufficiently mellowed by a tankard of ale, this lilting ballad:

> "I'd rather fight the bravest lads
>   That e'er came overseas,
> Than meet the blarsted Yankee Doodles
>   Among their rocks and trees."

So Batsto remained safe and its iron works continued until 1848. Batsto today is a mere turn in the shore road to Wading River, once called Bridgeport. Deriving its name from the Indian, Baatstoo, meaning a bathing place, you will find it a calm, peaceful cluster of houses now, dusted by the passing of speeding automobiles.

The first proprietor of the Batsto Estate was Israel Pemberton, who called the large, rambling manor house Whitcomb Manor. Pemberton sold the property to Charles Reed, who transferred it to Colonel Knox, who turned it over to Thomas Mayberry. In 1767 Joseph Ball purchased the place, town and surrounding lands, for the sum of fifty-five thousand pounds sterling.

Ball, during whose ownership Batsto became a place of importance as far as the Revolutionary War was concerned, was a practical fellow. He had his men clear many acres of the wild forest for cultivation. It was he who set up the blast furnace and began making a utility of the bog ore. Cannon and solid shot became the exclusive output during the war years.

Col. William Richards, who had served Washington with distinction, and who had been a warm personal friend of the Commander, was the next owner. The industry of Batsto prospered under his regime and when the war of

1812 came, the town again turned to making implements of war.

It was during this war that the colonel finished an order for fifty tons of cannon shot to be delivered in New York. The only ship in the river at the time had as its skipper Capt. David Mapps, a negro, who with a crew of his own race, traded regularly between the best-known ports of Jersey. David was a staunch Quaker.

One day Colonel Richards, anxious to get his cannon shot to the buyers, went down to the wharf and had Mapps called to the deck.

"David," said Richards, "I have a freight for you, and one that will pay you well."

Captain Mapps asked what it was.

"I want you to take a load of cannonballs to New York as soon as wind and tide will get you there."

"Did thee say cannonballs?" demanded the skipper.

The Colonel said he did and that the Government needed its ammunition badly.

"I'd like to oblige thee, Colonel," replied Captain Mapps, "but I cannot carry thy devil's pills that were made to kill people."

The ship left without the cannonballs.

Colonel Richards' management was succeeded by his son's in 1822. The son, Jesse, built and operated a glass works there for many years. The iron, glass, charcoal-burning, wood-sawing and teaming industries kept Batsto a center of lively activity with a host of workmen always on hand.

Jesse Richards was known for many miles around. He was an Episcopalian whose home was always open to circuit-riding ministers and any transients who happened to ride that way. When his Roman Catholic employes decided to erect a church at Pleasant Mills, he encouraged them and gave liberally to the cause.

It is in the tree-cloistered churchyard at Pleasant Mills that you will find Richards' grave, with its "Beloved, Honored, Mourned" inscription on the headstone.

The glass factory gave up at Batsto in 1865. In 1874 a fire broke out and before it was placed under control by the unorganized fire-fighting methods of the day, it had destroyed seventeen dwellings in the most historic part of the village. Now the venerable old manor house and lands surrounding it are part of the Wharton Estate.

Days of war, days when the refugees wandered the country, terrorizing the villages of the coast and pinelands, have little in common with days as they are now at The Forks, Batsto, and Tuckerton Landing. Down near the scene of the battle at Chestnut Neck, a monument immortalizes the memory of the patriots who fought, though outnumbered, and finally won. Near by is the fine old farm of the late Judge William C. French and his brother, Samuel T. French, a structure built on part of the old fortifications, a place for which some of the old trenches had to be cut down.

It is nothing for a cannonball or some trinket of yesteryear to be kicked up in the woods or fields hereabouts, from time to time.

Hosea Doughty, of Haddonfield, remembers walking near the old breastworks one day, long ago, when a stiff breeze was blowing in from the sea. Sand was blowing, too, and soon a cannonball and a buckle came into view. Many residents of Batsto and the shore towns below it have scores of such treasures unboastfully in their possession.

The old inn and store at Batsto recall the casual charm of other days, when stage passengers, soldiers, and women in hooped skirts, gathered there. The old mill stands today beside a sluggish sluiceway while behind it, along the Batsto River, below the dam, is the bed of slag from the ore diggings. A lake marks the site of the iron works itself, while atop the old manor house, dark within centuries of leafy shade, a watchman guards against the fires that often sweep the woodlands of their secrets.

There is much at Batsto that tells the town's historic story.

Batsto's hotel and company store. The scrip was issued more than a century ago at Batsto Works.

James Still, the Doctor of the Pines, and the tavern he renovated as home and office, near Medford.

III

THE DOCTOR OF THE PINES

In the pines they speak of him as "The Black Doctor." But the title they have bestowed by which to remember him is not one of disrespect.

They could as easily call him "The Doctor of the Pines," for that is what he was in days that were long ago. Probably no figure of backwoods country is greater revered or more graphically recalled.

James Still, "The Black Doctor," died in 1885. A man of great heart and compassion, with neither official title nor medical certificates, Dr. Still has been spoken of many thousands of times when his amazing cures were recalled.

At innumerable forgotten hamlets of the pinelands they will tell you, "Sure, I remember the Black Doctor. My people took me to see him when I was a boy. He cured my Aunt Mamie."

Only a few of us remember that Dr. Still wrote a book, an autobiography, published by J. B. Lippincott, of Philadelphia. This knowledge came back to light with the death of the doctor's only daughter, Lucretia, in November of 1930. The volume, published in 1877, eight years before the doctor's death, was among Lucretia's scattered effects.

It is from this book that the doctor's story is best told. He reveals himself a gentleman, overcoming the prejudices raised against him and educating himself in Letters and Medicine to a remarkable degree. In the preface of his autobiography he says that he was barred from the advantages of what we think of as education.

> It is very true [he confesses] that my parents were poor and unable to school their children as was also the case with many others in our section of the country. Their main object was to provide bread for us and they had reason to congratulate themselves on their success if they were thus fortunate.
>
> It so happened that I received three months' instruction in reading, writing and arithmetic, which completed me to start out in life. If so be I should prefer a professional life of any kind, as doctor, lawyer or minister, I stood robed with three months' education with which to start. For this much I feel truly thankful when I look around me and see so many deprived of even this.

Of his book, Dr. Still says:

> I know the critic will find fault and also laugh; but I ask him to put himself in my forlorn condition, and perhaps his sympathy will be excited for those less favored than himself. Let the case be as it may, I feel content to let it pass before the public for what it is worth. Perhaps I might have done better but my time has been very limited while engaged in work. I have written mostly at night, being busy through the day attending my practice.

And a practice Dr. Still could truthfully call it. Many of those taking a short-cut to upper shore resorts have passed Church Road across Marlton Pike to Vincentown and on. They have wondered perhaps what those two desolate buildings just beyond the pike could be. Here the wind has swept and the storm has poured its torrents without sign of inhabitant. The larger building, recently demolished, was the doctor's home. The tiny building adjoining was his office. Here patients, white and black, came for treatment and cure, from many miles around.

"I hope this book," Dr. Still has written, characteristically, "may be a stimulus to some poor, dejected fellow man who almost hopelessly sits down and folds his arms, saying 'I know nothing. I can do nothing.' "

Dr. Still was born in Washington Township, now Shamong, Burlington County, in 1812. The town was Indian Mills, the entirety of which was then owned by one Samuel Reeve. His father was Levin Still and his mother, Charity. Both of his parents were born in Maryland and both were slaves. Levin Still bought his freedom and then undertook to free his wife by bringing her to New Jersey. The couple settled at Indian Mills, where Levin sawed wood and chopped lumber for a living.

They lived here one year, during which time the doctor was born. Dr. Still recalls that his mother said he was born with two teeth, which, he explains, was taken as an ill foreboding. Then the family moved to Thompson Place, about a mile away, and remained there another year. They removed a second time to a house they shared with a colored man named Cato.

At the Cato place [says Dr. Still] I date my first recollections, being about two and a half years old. I recollect my father bringing me a pair of new shoes from Lumberton. At this place I also recollect first seeing a constable. His name was Israel Small. He was riding on horseback in pursuit of some one of the Milligan family which lived opposite to us, and so impressed was I by the terror of the law that I did not know at that time but that in the constable was vested all the power on the earth.

Here a brother of James was born. Dr. Still remembers women bustling about on that auspicious day, associated with the "taste of nice tea." The Still home at this time was "an old log house, one story high, and an attic, with one door, a large fireplace; no glass windows." There were two rooms on the first floor and one on the second. There were no stoves, no carpets. "Women wore short gowns and petticoats. Six or seven yards would make a gown to be worn on First Day," he recalls in passing.

It was after a Dr. Fort had visited the village that Dr. Still, yet a tiny black nondescript, decided he would be a doctor. The urge, he says, "took deep root in me, so deep that all the drought of poverty or lack of education could not destroy the desire.

"It grew with me and strengthened with my strength. My thinking faculties were aroused and I soon began to practise. Among the children I procured a piece of glass and made virus of spittle; I also procured a thin piece of pine bark which I substituted for a lancet." There followed ceremonial vaccinations.

After living with Cato over two years, James Still's father bought some land near by and built a house on it. The family increased at regular intervals and when the children were grown, some were put out with other families where there was no offspring. Older sisters went away first but James stayed at home, playing about the yard, observing many things and "looking forward to the time when I should be, like Dr. Fort, riding around healing the sick and doing great miracles." Later the youth made charcoal, split rails and picked cranberries in helping to support the family.

Hard times came. Dr. Still tells of one day when the starving house cat, Jacko, desperately snatched at a piece of meat.

"I sprang at him," he says, "caught him by the throat with one hand and took the meat out of his mouth with the other, placing it in my own. This poverty at times would cloud my vision when I looked forward to my most cherished hopes."

It was then that the few school days came. Dr. Still came to know other children for the first time. He did not like their sports. He could not shoot marbles. At baseball he was chosen always as scorekeeper.

"There was one thing I soon learned," wrote the physician of the pines, "that was to curse and swear, although this was never known to my parents. Our school books were the New Testament and Comley's Spelling Book." Here the pupils learned grammar and "everything useful" as well as to "pronounce improperly."

Charity, the boy's mother, was a staunch Methodist. His father preferred no denomination but was a great reader of Scriptures.

"I often thought," wrote Dr. Still, "that his whole soul was wrapped up in the twenty-fourth verse of the thirteenth chapter of Proverbs 'He that spareth the rod hateth his son; but he that loveth him, chastiseth him betimes.' "

The nearest neighbors to the Still's home were members of an Indian family, that of Job Moore. "His eldest son," Dr. Still says, "was named Job and he and I were very social. We played together and fished and hunted when opportunity would permit. My father was very strict with his children; we were not allowed to run about and play on Sundays like other children. All of us who could read must stay at home and read Scriptures. Those who could not read must study their spelling lesson. Believe me, Sunday was a very long day."

When James was ten his father bought a yoke of oxen and it became his lot, he says, to drive them. He was proud of this business at first and then it became a source of vexation. Wood was hauled to Medford and "the oxen were so slow I thought I should die of tire. In all this the sting of

Dr. Fort's lancet never left me. Oh, how many have lived and died without knowing anything of the rugged road the poor of the world have to travel!"

When James was eleven, his brother was put out to live with Aaron Engle and this day he puts down as one of great trial. "He was the eldest," he says, "and I always had something to lean upon, but now all was gone." Dr. Still began to read the Scriptures in earnest and any religious tracts he could get his hand upon. "I read by pine light. There was the open fire for illumination, for candles were not plenty.

I had a great love for truthfulness [he confesses] and was very fearful of the devil and ghosts, particularly at night. I was also afraid of Indian Job. He was a tall man, about six feet six inches tall, I think. He would often get drunk and go whooping about in Indian fashion, which was a great terror to me. Job was killed, finally. A wagon containing a cord and a quarter of green oak wood passed over him on one of his drunken frolics.

I recollect one night that his son, Job, and I were standing after meeting. We heard a shrill shout coming apparently from the graveyard, where old Job was buried. Young Job said to me, "That's Daddy." I trembled in every muscle and sweated from every pore.

We went to the meeting house and I watched the door and windows, expecting to see old Job enter but he did not come."

For a long time James Still lived in terrible fear of old Job's ghost.

Labor in and around Medford followed, chopping wood and doing odd jobs. James was careful of his possessions, which, of course, were few. All through his life, he never lost his pocket-knife. At last he was bound out to a farmer and given the job of digging potatoes and husking corn. In the evenings he played dominoes with the other workers. He did not like the game and when he left the farm, never played it again.

Here on the edge and in the midst of the pine country there was less despising of the blacks by the whites. James mingled freely with the white boys and wondered why the black people were looked down upon. He wondered why the same great God had made the same races of different colors and dwelled on that portion of the Acts of the Apostles which reads, "God hath made of one blood all nations of men." Many things bewildered, puzzled him.

Was this wiry, angular black boy ever to be a physician? Was this nobody, brought up in the backwoods, ever to realize his dream, to become a doctor, to be like Dr. Fort, to triumph over his poverty, his hardships, his color, to become "The Black Doctor," beloved physican of the pines? It did not seem so. And yet, despite the cruel whippings his father gave him, through all that time when he was bound out again, his soul sang. It was a sad song but a determined one, a song fashioned to make dreams come true.

It was provided that when James became twenty-one, Amos Wilkins, to whom he was last bound out, was to give to Levin Still, the boy's father, ten dollars in cash and a new suit. It was also part of the bargain that he should be permitted to go to school one month each winter. He stayed with Wilkins three years and fulfilled the agreement with one exception: It was Wilkins' principle to give his help a dram of liquor every morning; James didn't like the taste and poured it out.

Just before his twenty-first birthday, Still was hurt. Horses he was driving became frightened and ran away. He was thrown from his seat and the wagon ran over him. However, he recovered in time for the big day. Having arrived at man's estate, he tied all his belongings in two cotton handkerchiefs, took his money, ten dollars, and started out for Philadelphia. Taking back roads so as not to be seen by the too curious, the boy arrived at his sister's home and next day obtained a job in a glue factory at ten dollars a month. He at once opened a savings account, his mind and heart set on the one great goal.

At twenty-two he had saved a hundred dollars and had fallen in love with a slender colored girl, Angelina Willow. Long ago he had determined that he would never marry until he was established in the medical profession, but as is often the case, love was too strong.

In speaking of his courtship of Angelina, Dr. Still muses on a curious anecdote. He writes that he had become quite a singer, so with a few spare pennies he purchased four love songs. He sang them. Angelina sang them. And so they were married. Their married bliss was brief, however. After the arrival of a baby, Beulah, Angelina contracted tuberculosis and died. Beulah was entrusted to the care of Still's mother and James lived by himself, chopping wood, digging marl and doing any work that was to be had. He had procured some medical books and read them constantly.

Into James's life came Henrietta Thomas, another colored girl—homeless, friendless, and an orphan, in much the same standing as was Still himself. He had married Henrietta just before he had news from his mother that little Beulah had died. He bought four acres and cleared the land around his new home. He bought a cow and built a small barn. Events at this time came in quick succession. Little Jimmie, Jr., arrived, old Levin died, and his son was left a patrimony, which, when all debts were paid, amounted to nothing at all.

Not long after that, James Still began to make medicines. He bought a horse, a still, and learned to brew strange mixtures. He began to hunt for sassafras roots with which to concoct weird remedies, sold in surrounding towns with considerable success. James Still began to be known to a small circle as "the doctor." Pouring over his yellowed books, he then ventured into the making of all sorts of salves and remedial concoctions, using extracts and herbs.

Charles and William Ellis, Philadelphia pharmacists, were interested in the stories of cures which began to emanate from the pine towns and the other villages near Medford where Dr. Still operated. They definitely contracted to buy his "cures" and with the money he earned, Still was able to buy more ingredients.

One of his first "cases" was scrofula from which a neighbor's daughter was suffering. She had been treated by a local physician for some time without result. After Dr. Still had supplied his sassafras remedy the girl was not long in getting well.

Every now and then James Still thought he would like to have definite medical training and a certificate to hang on his wall. He wanted an official M. D. But when he spoke of his aspirations he was ridiculed so much that he made such suggestions at rare intervals.

"Who ever heard of a black doctor?" they asked. He decided that he had better go on in the other way.

There was in the neighborhood a wooden mortar and an Indian pestle. Thomas Cline, who owned them, willingly loaned them to Still, who began to find himself a very busy man. His reputation with the Philadelphia druggists grew. Henrietta helped him but even so he had more than he could do. A man by the name of Abraham Corson had to be employed, finally, to do the actual digging for roots.

Another test came in the case of a daughter of John Miller. It was again chronic scrofula. The girl had become so seriously ill that her condition was offensive to the rest of her family. Miller came to Dr. Still and told him if he could cure the disease he could cure anything.

Coming to Still in such condition that she could not raise her hand to her head, the victim left him in ten days able to comb her own hair. The added prestige of the case made a wagon indispensable, so Still made one himself.

Local physicians began to take notice. They laughed, Still says, as he went along in his rough carryall, a cigarbox his medicine chest. Then they laughed no longer but took measures to have his business stopped. He was practising, they said, without a license. But he had been careful, accepting only what people thought they ought to give him. There had been no fixed rates. Just the same these other doctors said they had grounds for a protest. Still consulted an attorney and found he could circumvent the law by charging merely for "delivery of medicine."

"The Black Doctor" became a byword. Unusual cases always called for his services. No hour was too late, no town too far away. Dr. Still always prayed in the presence of the patient before treating a case, asking for divine knowledge of how to seek a cure. Soon he had paid off the one hundred and sixty dollar mortgage on his property, discarding the old, rickety wagon and buying a more comfortable carriage.

In 1849 Dr. Still moved into a comfortable and auspicious-looking house next door to a tavern-keeper who had laughed with the others at the doctor's beginnings. Later he bought the tavern property itself for one thousand nine hundred and seventy-five dollars. He had no great amount of money, but he gave a mortgage against all that he owned, so sure was he of success, credentials or no credentials. Dr. Still paid off his mortgage in a few years. He used the renovated tavern property as a headquarters until his death. Near the crossroad at Marlton Pike and Church Road many have passed by this building and its adjacent office, without knowing anything of "The Black Doctor" himself.

Dr. Still had a penchant for building. Much of his thought when he was not attending patients was given to the planning and erection of many buildings on his property.

As it has been frequently said that I know nothing of fevers [he wrote], especially by physicians, I feel it incumbent upon me to give a brief sketch of my treatment. It has always been my impression that the doctor was sent for to prevent protraction of disease, and by proper remedies to alleviate the suffering of the patient. Such being the case, my duty seemed plain.

If the head be hot, take whisky, vinegar, and soft water (one teacup of each). Soak the feet at night in ashes and warm water. Give patient a dose of vegetable physic every day or every other day, according to circumstances.

Dr. Still repeatedly pointed out that at no time did he take a uniform cure for a specific disease, rather suiting the tonic and medicine to the individual he was treating.

In his book many recipes, concoctions, and prescriptions have been listed, mostly made from combining ipecac, saffron, camphor, Virginia snakeroot, pleurisy root, as well as many other ingredients in their "proper quantities, all properly bruised." Sudorific drops, emetic powders, antibilious

powders and cough balsam were among the many remedies
Dr. Still produced, hopeful of passing them on.

In the last days Dr. Still was no longer able to make his
way to Medford, Red Lion, Beaverville, Buddtown,
Friendship, Chairville, Hampton Gate, and Indian Mills,
his old homestead. He had suffered a stroke, and kept himself mostly indoors or on the porch of his office. To him
here, toward the end, came many hundreds of blacks and
whites, some of them the very physicians who had laughed
at him, for treatment, advice, and cures.

Cancers, tumors, and mysterious maladies seemed to be
his forte, and there are many in the pines who will tell you
that "The Black Doctor" saved their lives.

> When I take a retrospective view of my life [he wrote in con-
> cluding] of the many difficulties with which I have had to con-
> tend, the mountains of prejudice which I have had to meet, the
> poverty which hung as a dark cloud about my childhood and
> early manhood, without training, a mind uncultivated and undis-
> ciplined, no one to lend a helping hand but many to give a cold
> shoulder and hinder my progress as best they could, I almost
> wonder that I attained my present time of calm weather and clear
> sky. All the blessings and many of the luxuries of life surround
> me, and as I humbly trust I have served in some measure the gen-
> eration to which I belong, I can only exclaim, "He that is mighty
> hath done great things for me."

Here and there through the book there are many philos-
ophies and whimsical observations. "The Black Doctor"
remembers collecting many curious and freak animals. He
took an uncommon interest in children and their sicknesses,
curing a great many, never permitting any employe to prepare their medicines. He had little time for a man who
would not pay his debts.

Once he took time to attend the funeral of his old

"owner," Amos Wilkins. He sent his own children regularly to school, but they were later excluded from classes, when their teacher became suddenly persuaded that it was a sin to teach colored pupils. Mrs. Still died long before she could enjoy the full fruit of the prosperous years.

A visit to the Centennial, medical and social visits from old schoolmates, and these writings by the dim light of his office, seem to have given a lonely happiness to the old man. One son went elsewhere, seeking reputation, they say, much as his father had done. The second physician of the Still family failed, to die, several years ago, in an almshouse.

Every now and then Dr. Still indicated in his writings that he dabbled in rhymes. His effects, they say, contained several Bibles, many priceless medical books and volumes of poetry. But there was nothing poetic about the old house, as we found it a few years ago. Somebody had been using the backyard for a dump of trash and tin cans. Someone else had been staging a smashing spree in one of the back rooms, wrecking forever the memories an old house had of the Physician of the Pines. Now the place is gone altogether.

All Dr. Still's life seems to be summed up in a long, rhythmic sing-song, "Nobody's Song," which he has included in his memoirs. Perhaps Dr. Still wrote it himself. If we ever get time, we are going to write some music for it with a strumming accompaniment:

> I am thinking just now of nobody
> And all that nobody's done.
> For I've a passion for nobody
> That nobody else would own.
> I bear the name of nobody,
> For from nobody I sprung.
> And I sing the praise of nobody
> As nobody mine has done.

In life's young morning nobody
To me was tender and dear
And my cradle was rocked by nobody
For nobody was ever near.
I was petted and praised by nobody
And nobody brought me up.
And when I was hungry nobody
Gave me to drink and sup.

I went to school to nobody,
And nobody taught me to read.
I played in the streets with nobody
And nobody ever gave heed.
I recounted my tale to nobody
For nobody was willing to hear,
And my heart it clung to nobody
And nobody to shed a tear.

And when I grew older, nobody
Gave me a helping turn.
And by the good aid of nobody,
I began my living to earn.
And hence I courted nobody
And said I'd nobody's be,
I asked to marry nobody
And nobody married me.

Thus I trudged with nobody
And nobody cheers my life.
I have a love for nobody
Which nobody has for his wife.
So here's a health to nobody
For nobody's now in town,
And I've a passion for nobody
That nobody else would own.

IV

SPEEDWELL

South of Chatsworth and Jones Mill and beyond the blackened acres that were pines before the fire of several years ago, is Speedwell, or as it was originally known, Speedwell Furnace.

The road to Speedwell is a dreary one. It winds and twists through charred stumps and stunted trees. After leaving Chatsworth we found no habitation of any kind. The landscape stretches out as far as the eye can see, a panorama of broken wilderness.

On the road to Speedwell there is a corner known as Tom's Grave. It is a scraggly crossroads, a cow path that perhaps leads eventually to the site of the old hotel at Eagle. But here in the "L" of the intersection is a little mound, surrounded by undergrowth and swampy muck. This is "Tom's Grave."

Nobody knows who Tom was. He was colored, the story goes, and he was found stiff and staring one morning in the middle of the road. At any other crossroads in the world, perhaps, he might have been the victim of a hit-run driver, but not on the road to Speedwell.

No one had ever seen the fellow before. He was fairly well dressed but there was nothing to identify him among the limited effects found on his person.

There was little excitement. At length somebody conceived the idea of naming the dead man "Tom" and burying him on the spot. So they laid him to rest, marked the place with a rude cross and called the corner "Tom's Grave." The marker has fallen away, but they showed us the approximate place where the burial was made.

Near by, further up the road, are "Jake's Spring" and Burnt Bridge, which to those who live thereabouts are landmarks with their own stories. But just who Jake was and what occasion gave the bridge its adjective, are legends that have faded in much retelling.

If you had entered the clearing that surrounds Speedwell a few years ago, you would have been in time to see the old Indian schoolhouse. The little log building was about fourteen feet square. It had one story and low ceilings and cedar shingles, mossed and rotting. At one end of the single room was a huge fireplace, fully one-third the size of the school.

Even the oldest inhabitants of the section do not know when it was built. They do know, however, that as far as their memories go back, it has been called the Indian schoolhouse. Of course, it is well-known that years ago this section was the home of the Edge-Pollocks, a part of the Delaware tribe. It is not unusual, even now, to find arrowheads and tomahawks through this whole vicinity.

The legend is that the schoolhouse was originally erected to give joint education to the children of white settlers and those of the few Indians who still roamed the country when it was built. Not more than twelve or fifteen pupils could have been accommodated. After serving as a school, the cabin, for it was no more than that, became a blacksmith shop. Today the school is just another ruin of the pinelands, with here and there a wheel or wagon part in the clearing, to recall its last activity.

Schooldays were unusual in old Speedwell Furnace. Folk

in the vicinity will tell you that it was difficult to get children to attend school because parents themselves did not see the necessity of education. The argument was, as we heard it, that parents had gone thus far without "larnin'" and that they couldn't see much necessity in urging their children to "take to any."

Speedwell's iron furnace differed little in appearance and operation from other iron furnaces of the pine towns. The lowlands from which bog ore could be procured was the first necessity, and of this swamp ground there is much in and about Speedwell. Where most of the ore was obtained has now become a beautiful lake, favorite of renowned fishermen.

All that remains of the old furnace is a portion of a stone wall, not more than four feet in height. A few stones protrude from the marshy ground near by. Older residents say that the furnace was more than twenty feet high. Near the ruin is the usual pile of slag, the residue of the ore after the smelting. All is grown over by a mass of trees and undergrowth.

You will not readily forget Speedwell. Once a town, its "community" was reduced to but one house, the home of Mr. and Mrs. Stephen Lee. Lee, smiling and soft-spoken, and his wife, always delighted if she can provide a little "snack" from her kitchen for you, conduct a boys' camp.

Speedwell is an oasis in the barrens of South Jersey's hinterland. Everything is memory, days of long ago, days when liquor sold at the old Eagle Hotel for six and one-quarter cents a drink, where a meal cost two "levees" of twelve and one-half cents each.

The day we were there we stopped to talk with one Piney not far down the road. Noting the desolation and wondering, as everyone must do, how people live in the backwoods, we said:

"You must have a rough time of it here, getting along."

"No," he answered us, "you see, I don't own no land. I just live here."

Apparently to own property is to be poorer, at Speedwell.

Prospertown once enjoyed its location near the Mount Holly-Freehold Post Road, a principal roadway when the Continentals mustered for the Battle of Monmouth.

V

PROSPERTOWN, ARCHER'S CORNER, COLLIER'S MILL

ON A narrow ribbon of a road that plunges from the border of Monmouth County to the Ocean County pines, there are three points deserving names upon the modern maps. The first is Prospertown; the second, Archer's Corner; and the third, Collier's Mill.

Archer's Corner maintains its identity because a main State highway passes through it, en route to Lakewood and the shore. Prospertown and Collier's Mill, their heydays forgotten, are quickly pursuing their memories of prosperous times.

On a map of New Jersey you will see that along the northwest border of Ocean County, the boundary follows a road that cuts almost directly from Mt. Holly to Freehold. It is obviously the most direct route, passing through Jobstown, Prospertown, Burksville, Smithburg and Elton, tiny villages hardly familiar to any but their inhabitants. This, a century back, was the Mt. Holly-Freehold Post Road.

Time and again there have been moves to improve the route but as often it was discovered that there were no influential residents along the line to secure definite action. Recently there was no highway, but rather a winding wagon-track passing mostly through open country.

Following the division into East and West Jersey, this

road was one of the first. It was still a serviceable and principal roadway when the Continentals mustered for the Battle of Monmouth. Pausing at Prospertown, they found a country hotel, a cluster of homes, and a grain mill.

There was a warming fire, with plenty of ale at the inn, the miller probably had a family of personable daughters and the little lake that furnished power for the mill must have provided an atmosphere for romance.

The homes left in Prospertown now are up the road from the old hotel and the mill. Despite the fact that most of them are unpainted, a few being painted on but one side, they may have had no connection with this erstwhile center of town. For here all is neglect, loneliness and desolation.

The hotel is unoccupied. Its door is gone. Its upper windows are tightly shuttered. A shout inside echoes through the unpapered, dark, and clammy rooms. In the gloom of the lower cubicles one can see bales of straw. Someone is apparently using the place for a stable. There is nothing to invite even the most travel-spent guest.

What is left of the mill is across the road. A tall, gaunt and shattered building, it leans precariously toward the water beyond the spillway. There are holes in its frame walls and so there should be: the wood, hewn by hand from the surrounding pinelands, is more than a century old. Inside there are great beams, rusted machinery, and rotting boards. The floors are gone. The cooing of a wood dove, from high in the rickety frame, is followed by the plop of fragments in the stagnant pools of rainwater under the crumbling sluiceway.

No one seems to know just when the mill was established. The water of the lake, larger in days gone by, comes from the Ivanhoe Brook. The water splashes down over the dam, plunging on, forgetful of the years when there was a Post Office and general store, long since destroyed by fire.

Beyond the crossroads, where the trail cuts over the old Monmouth Road, there are two or three occupied houses to constitute the village.

We had heard a report that here at Prospertown, of all places, they drilled for oil not long ago. A man was meandering in the clearing back of one of the weather-beaten, unpainted dwellings, poking among discarded plows and tools and chicken-coops. We asked him about it.

"Yes," said he, in the usual slow drawl, "they dug for oil right over there. Somebody had an idea there was plenty of it. But there warn't none at all."

He pointed to a portion of the drill used, beside his unofficial outdoor museum, and then motioned to a little open space at the edge of the woods across the road. This was the place where reports of an oil strike had brought hundreds of people, Pineys and constables, mayors and experts, flocking to see what was doing. Nothing happened.

Leaving Prospertown, you may find the road rough going, over green marl and at intervals, lumps of Jersey sandstone. Passing beyond Archer's Corner, you come upon a better highway. Then suddenly, you are before a large, wintry-looking house. This is Collier's Mill, the Collier's Mill of today.

Years ago, when sawmills and smelters' furnaces employed hundreds of workers through the pinelands, Collier's Mill was a center of activity and merrymaking. Collier's Mill did not get its name from a founder named Collier as many persons have believed but rather from the fact that its early days were prosperous for charcoal burners. A charcoal maker was a collier just as much as the man who digs deep in the earth for anthracite fuel.

Of the palmy days of Collier's Mill, information comes only through tradition and hearsay. The best-known name seems to be that of "Eph" Empson, whose family must have been the town's pioneers. Old "Eph" was well known as a man of ability and enterprise throughout the countryside.

At Collier's Mill, a stream of water known as Borden's Mill Branch was dammed for power and here a sawmill was established. Collier's Mill Pond soon became a paradise for wild fowl, particularly geese and ducks. "Eph" Empson made it a rule, to be observed by his family and employes, that all bird life should be protected. For many years all game birds made Collier's Mill a haven. Old "Eph" could walk along the pond without disturbing them.

Borden's Mill Branch empties into Harrison Pond, Head of Snag, Elisher Harris, Oblanon, Ridgeway and Shannon Brook, as well as other smaller waterways each with their special name, on its way to the Toms River. Empson cleared the swamps and soon was growing cranberries where there had been nothing but worthless bogs.

As the town grew, a store, a school, a Post Office and a church were built. Around them came new log and frame homes. Empson was proud of his town as the community became an active center. There were dances on Saturday nights and the most famous of the Jersey pine fiddlers made the dance hall echo with music and shrill cries. Those were days when enthusiasm came in bottles.

"Eph" Empson was a horse fancier. In his day he constructed two race tracks with stables for his famous horses. One track, down the road toward Archer's Corner, may be discovered even now, out through an orchard planted there later. But the track below the old Empson mansion is lost forever. The stables, some of them, are still standing. They are used as cranberry sorting houses now.

The school is gone. The store and Post Office building provide neither groceries nor mails. The store is a dark cavernous place, with shelves full of cobwebs. Upon the butcher's block there is a rusted cleaver. A lantern swings, globeless, from the ceiling.

Only a couple of families call Collier's Mill home in these days and you have to hunt them. The only people we saw there were Ivins Grant and his grandson. Ivins, a grizzled, white-whiskered old man, was spryly chopping a windfall tree. Grant remembered old "Eph" Empson well, and why shouldn't he?

"Pretty used to the place now," he said, speaking for himself. "Been here for fifty-two years."

Grant, one of the last employes of Empson, by whose estate he is still employed, remembers the gay days, the dances, the hustle and bustle of the time when Collier's Mill was a real town.

"Now," he said, "people come only in the summer. They like to swim in the cedar water. One fellow was drowned right down there couple of years ago."

"Eph" Empson was a well-known figure, Grant recalls, for the Governor appointed him a judge during his middle years. He presided in court at Toms River and filled many important posts to which he was later elected.

Empson's horse was his undoing, Ivins Grant recalled. In his latter days, days of driving along country roads in a shining carriage, Empson hitched a particularly spirited mount to his carryall. He was thrown to his death when the animal hauled the vehicle off the road, upsetting it among some stumps.

With the death of "Uncle Eph" and with his wife and family moving from Collier's Mill, the town seems to have stood still. The wild ducks and geese left the pond when they found it unprotected, the sawmill fell into decay, the store closed and the church became the scene of only occasional services. The village was once reported as the headquarters of the Ku Klux Klan.

Grant lives on the third floor of the store building.

"It's not so good," he complained. "I'm getting too old to go climbing two flights of stairs all the time."

On a sunny day the prospect at Collier's Mill is cheery enough but in the rain it is a dismal corner. From the ponds there rises a cold, chilling mist, a haze that curtains the countryside, making it dim and far away.

The shutters on the old mansion bang in the wind like eerie handclappings, weird echoes of the days when hoopskirts rustled through its rooms. The roof leaks and across the front porch there rests a giant walnut tree, tired of standing upright and surrendering at last to the wind that swirls around the eaves.

Old Ivins Grant wiped his spectacles and leaning on his ax, wondered how much of his fifty-third year there would be required for taking the old tree down, removing forever another landmark of Collier's Mill.

VI

LOVELADIES AND PEAHALA

Loveladies.

Peahala.

What names for towns, you say. Who were the ladies and were they in love? Or did some sailorman admire them so frankly that he named this seacoast town forever in their memory? And Peahala—does such a place really have existence and does its name have meaning?

Come down to the shore for a while. Here in the tang of salt air, here to the south of old Barnegat Light where the spume is swishing up the island beach, let's sit on a dune and talk about these two old villages.

Up there, to the north—see those little huts and the white Coast Guard station beyond them? That's all there is of Loveladies now. And down there where the beach swerves in a bit, where the sand is flecked with the ribs of old wrecked ships—that's Peahala. But here there are memories of wars and shipburnings and hoopskirted women who watched exciting happenings from upper windows in towns that are no longer.

Loveladies, sad to say, has no such amorous meaning as might better serve our story. Originally an isolated sand bar with no Manahawkin bridge to link it with the shore, it was named Loveladies Island, after the man who is supposed to have obtained it as a grant from a British sovereign. Of that there is little known, although at Peahala history is more definitely established.

At Loveladies where, except in summer, the sand crunches to only the measured tread of the Coast Guard watchman, where Captain Charles Norris Cramer once kept a wary eye open for liquor smugglers, there were once scenes of more open, more honest conflict. During the war of 1812, Ocean County vessels trading to New York found their trade seriously handicapped by British cruisers along the coast. Occasionally some bold, fortunate master would elude enemy vigilance to arrive in port safely. But fortune seldom smiled.

Commodore Hardy in his flagship, the *Ramillus*, flanked by seventy-four guns, had command of the British blockading squadron along the New Jersey waters. From all accounts, actual and traditional, he was one of the most honorable officers in the British service. Unlike the infamous Admiral Cockburn, who commanded the blockading squadron further to the south, Hardy never took private American property, unless it was contraband of war, without at least offering compensation.

Hardy's vigilance inflicted considerable damage on American coasters, however, holding up lumber shipments to and from the Jersey towns. In his *Ramillus* he came close to Barnegat Inlet, and sent in many barges loaded to the gunwales with armed men. At one time he made for two American ships anchored in the inlet, boarding the schooner *Greyhound*, with Captain Jesse Rogers, of Potter's Creek, in command, attempting to take her out to sea. When she grounded, the British set her afire. She went down with her cargo.

The invaders, it is recorded, later set fire to a sloop belonging to Captain Jonathan Winner, Hezekia Soper, and Timothy Soper of Waretown. But war—real war, with two great powers at conflict—was, as far as Jersey's coast was concerned, a game, an outdoor sport, in those days. If you lived in Waretown, in Loveladies, in Peahala or thereabouts, you could get a ringside seat by climbing to a housetop, first taking the precaution to send your children into the woods, out of the way. It is a question whether it was the war or the unobstructed view that mattered to the observers.

This Waretown sloop, either the *Mary Elizabeth* or the *Susan*, was saved when Commodore Hardy sent up flares that there was more valuable cargo and infinitely more sport further out to sea. So the barges retired, but not before a landing party had come ashore on the south side of the island, to kill and make away with fifteen head of cattle owned by Jeremiah Spragg and John Allen.

The owners were away. But the rules of war in those days demanded that those who killed the cattle of private persons must at least promise to pay. That's what these Britishers did. They left word that if the owners would present their bill to Hardy they could collect forthwith. But, though the War of 1812 was unpopular in New Jersey, the shore citizenry always displayed too much patriotism to accept money from the enemy.

At another time the schooner *President*, with Captain Amos Birdsall of Waretown, bound for New York, was taken by Hardy, who at once began to junk the ship, ripping up deck planking and pulling down masts to be sawed. Captain Birdsall and his crew, however, were allowed the freedom of the decks. They were also given permission to leave in the yawl and make for shore, but this trip was postponed several times by mutual understanding because of the heavy sea. Finally Birdsall and his men returned home on a fishing smack, having been, in modern jargon, hijacked.

Captain Thomas Bunnell had his adventures, too. Master of the sloop *Elizabeth*, and hailing from Forked River, he and his vessel were taken in charge by two barges sent in from the British fleet off Loveladies. The *Elizabeth* was towed to sea but was lost off Long Island a few days later. Bunnell returned home on a neutral Spanish ship upon which he had been deposited with all courtesy by the British seamen.

They tell the story of how the shooting of one British tar almost started war in earnest off Loveladies Island. The sloop *Traveler* had been set afire under the nose of a Captain Grant. The *Maria*, Captain Joshua Warren, and the *Friendship*, Captain Thomas Mills, two more ships of the same size, dodged up the inlet for shelter but Hardy sent two barges to board and plunder them.

One barge made for the *Friendship*. As the bowsman caught hold of the taffrail to make her fast, Jesse Chadwick, a Revolutionary soldier on leave, ripped out his pistol and shot him. The bowsman screamed and fell into the water. All decent warfare ended right there. The barges withdrew to the fleet, which opened fire on the sloop, sending in more than two hundred balls, only a few of which had any effect.

At Forked River, war was often a most remarkable gentleman's conflict to be witnessed from housetops. One house in particular, that of Charles Parker, father of a New Jersey Governor, Joel Parker, didn't get finished very quickly because citizens were always climbing up on the roof with the carpenters to see the battle's progress.

It was here along Loveladies Island and on the mainland shore that the first draft-dodgers became known. In order to raise troops, a draft was ordered through the dune villages. One man in every seven was to be called. But a plan was evolved that stopped the army leaders. Seven men would repeatedly club together and hire a substitute for a mere fifty dollars.

Those who were drafted were mostly despatched to the defense of Sandy Hook, where there was more grumbling over the horse-beef of the army commissary than actual fighting.

Wars have come and wars have gone since then. Houses of Loveladies, if ever there were many of them, have disappeared in the sand and beach brush and raging tides. In their place is the cluster of huts in among the dunes, where Coast Guarders live in simplicity with their families. If ever there was primitive peace it is here.

At Peahala, a club operated for accommodation of fishermen and gunners was the unofficial and seasonally used "city hall." A Professor Thomas, of Mt. Holly, long-deceased, held a deed, it is said, for Peahala Beach even while New Jersey was a British Colony, granted by George III. However, the property was taken from him after the war with England and the grant declared illegal.

Peahala is a headquarters of what for many years was known as one of the ocean's graveyards. Under the sands of the beach are wrecks of coasters and foreign ships, victims of nor'easters. One by one the old rotting frames come to light and disappear. Sand gives way to wind and wood to native firesides.

Here the storms of centuries have wrought their worst.

Here when the sea and wind are clashing, only a fool will launch a surf-boat. Barnegat Light, undermined by the slipping shore, shines through the darkness.

The beach patrol of Cramer's men was an all-day, all-night watch. The patrol-boat, equipped with machine guns and high-powered rifles, clocks to punch, towers to spy from, guarding against the landing of rum—all these replaced the pirates of Barnegat, cutthroats who, tradition says, watched their chance to sneak ashore and bury their spoils. History has repeated itself, perhaps! Along the Jersey shore it again pitted gallant men against sly methods of the outlaw.

Few wrecks have been tossed up here in recent years. A wise pilot gives this bit of desolation a wide berth. In his mind's eye he sees those skeleton ships in the sand, those houses placed too near the sea.

Summer homes are increasing about Peahala. Here, at least, is little of the sequestered silence of Loveladies. If there were ladies, they have loved and laughed and gone away.

Oyster Creek, above Leeds' Point, named for Daniel Leeds, first surveyor-general of West Jersey, member of the New Jersey Council until 1708, and early publisher of almanacs in Philadelphia.

VII

NEW EGYPT

"And the seven years of plenteousness . . . were ended.
. . . and the dearth was in all lands; but in all the land
of Egypt there was bread . . . and the famine was
over all the face of the earth; and Joseph opened all
the store-houses and sold unto the Egyptians . . .
and all the countries came into Egypt to Joseph to
buy corn; because that the famine was so sore in
all lands."

—GENESIS

ONCE upon a time there was a town called Timmins' Mill.

You can scan your map of New Jersey from north to
south and east to west but you won't find it—because it
isn't there any more.

And yet, in the 1700's, Timmins' Mill was the geographical center of New Jersey and an important town. It was a
mill town and the mill was owned by Timmins who held
title, they say, to the whole village.

Timmins' Mill is still the State's approximate geographical center but it is no longer Timmins' Mill. It is New
Egypt now.

Mention Egypt and you think of the Nile, waving palms,
the Sphinx, and the Pyramids. You recall the story of Joseph, how he interpreted the dreams of the chief butler,
then the chief baker, and finally of Pharaoh himself.

The story of Joseph's adventures has a direct bearing on
how Timmins' Mill became New Egypt.

Joseph interpreted the chief butler's dream as meaning

that he would be restored to his official position. Then he told the chief baker that Pharaoh would cut off his head. His batting average on divining the meanings of dreams was five hundred when Pharaoh sent for him to get an interpretation of one of his own.

Pharaoh told how he had seen in his vision a stalk of corn on which there were seven good and seven bad ears. Joseph promptly revealed that this vision augured that there would be seven years of plenty and then seven years of famine. His interpretation came true and he was given a permanent appointment to Pharaoh's household as a sort of glorified major-domo. On his advice Egypt began to store away corn and when the famine came, it had plenty—so much, in fact, that it supplied many countries outside.

The story runs that in the neighborhood of Timmins' Mill at seeding time, there came an unequalled scarcity of seed corn. "Old Man Timmins" had for some reason put away a heavy stock. He had filled his mill, his barns and the storehouses of other people for miles around. Soon farmers came for seed corn, unable to procure it elsewhere. So Timmins' Mill became New Egypt.

There is another legend that has to do with the naming of New Egypt although it has no official stamp as has the other.

Many residents of the borderland between Burlington and Ocean Counties (New Egypt is just over the Ocean County border) recall a man named Haas who was a superintendent of schools. He married into one of the best-known families in this section, the Copes.

George B. Cope had come there from Bucks County, Pennsylvania, bringing a large family of boys and girls.

New Egypt, old Timmins' Mill, still retains some of the quaintness of Colonial times. The first Mormon sermon in Ocean County was preached at New Egypt, and Joseph Smith himself is said to have visited the village.

Pleasant Mills of Sweetwater, the last of several paper mills to occupy the site of the first mill, the cotton textile factory built by William Lippincott of Philadelphia in 1821. Across the road from the mill is the old Elijah Clark mansion, or "Kate Aylesford House." In the churchyard lie many early settlers and members of the Richards family.

These have grown up now and are well-known in Atlantic City and the Delaware Water Gap section where many are hotel operators. Cope had made a lot of money, they of New Egypt say, and had come to the Jersey Pines to invest it.

Haas married one of the Cope girls who for a time taught school in a village near New Egypt, Cranberry Hall. At school, one day, he was demonstrating spelling by syllables. For some reason, he wrote the name "New Egypt" on the blackboard and asked that the pupils of the one-room school divide.it into syllables. One bright boy stepped up and pronounced "New Egg Wiped" and was promptly reprimanded.

Long years after, some of the pupils recalled, with the rechristening of Timmins' Mill, how Haas had written "New Egypt" on the board.

They tell another story, one about old Timmins, in New Egypt, which is worth retelling here. Pay for grinding a grist was not made in cash, but by the miller's taking a toll of one-tenth of the load. Three hands were working in the mill. They had been warned that the toll must be taken, under penalty of dismissal. All three hands, they say, took the toll more than once, just to be sure Timmins' orders were carried out.

The grists were carried to New Egypt by horseback in former times, by oxen and by mule team. They came from Prospertown, Goshen, Irish Mills, Bucksburg (now Lakewood), Squankum, Blue Bell, Shelltown and Arneytown. Mills were then operating at such places as Recklesstown, Walnford, Cookstown, Hornerstown, Colliers', Blacks', Bennetts', Jacksons', and Francis'. The prestige of New Egypt as a milling center soon dwindled.

Timmins died and after several changes in ownership, the property became that of Morris E. Lamb, its owner when we went exploring there. Lamb expended a large amount of money for the erection of a new dam.

Timmins' Mill and not New Egypt is the forgotten town. Today in New Egypt there are approximately one thousand souls, all conveniences, a water system, electricity, a number of factories, a weekly newspaper, four churches, and a modern bank.

New Egypt remembers the land of pyramids with more than its name. There is a motion picture theatre, named for Isis, goddess of the Nile. And there is a Pyramid Masonic Lodge!

Recently the town specialized in summer boarding. There are three hotels and some twenty boarding-houses. Near by are numerous poultry farms and cranberry bogs.

New Egypt has always boasted giant hogs. Claims are made that on its fertile farms have been fattened the largest hogs the world has known. One recent specimen tipped the scales at one thousand and sixty-one pounds.

New Egypt used to boast a champion hog killer, Henry Hankins, a Civil War veteran, who claimed to have killed, prior to his retirement, a total of 74,250 hogs. He used to tell how he could dress three a minute, so adept was his skill.

Perhaps this story can be classed with that of the giant watermelon of Ong's Hat.

VIII

THE TUCKERTON ROAD

Maps are provoking. In many cases, if you examine one that is new and up-to-date, you will find more towns and villages, more creeks, swamps and roadways than are indicated on those with edges yellowed by sun and time.

Down in the bog country, however, in this pine country of Southern New Jersey, maps, like many other things, work in reverse. One that is modern may perchance contain a faint line, swerving from the old Marlton Pike above Marlton and curving toward the south, eventually finding Tuckerton by a back way. On an older edition the same road will be shown as a substantial highway.

So it should be. In spite of any skepticism haunting you after you have followed the outline of this pathway through wilds and woodlands that conceal it today, please believe that this was the old Tuckerton Stage Road, a route of bustling commerce, earnest passengers and "life that still had its thrills."

To find the road now you must shove off to the right at the second abrupt turn above Marlton. Where the older paved road veers sharply toward the left and Medford, the Tuckerton Road, marked by signboards from which the weather has erased all vestige of inscriptions, plunges straight on.

On this corner is the weather-beaten and bell-less Pine Grove Union Church. Services are held each Sunday. This building, it is said, was remodeled in 1906. We discovered, when we were there, that the floor inside sags a little already. Around the walls are certificates of those who signed a Lincoln-Lee Legion Pledge, an oath of Temperance. There are about thirty worshippers on the registered roll.

Continuing down the road a mile or so, there are two farmhouses, facing each other. They seem to nod knowingly, ruefully perhaps, as the adventure-seeking motorist presses on. The farm at the left, one of those owned by the Wilkins Brothers, descendants of a family which has held it for generations, is on the site of an old Indian encampment. Its present tenants do not know how old their house is, but they showed us proudly that its clapboards are hand-hewn and that pegs, instead of nails, hold it together.

At the farm across the way its owner, Jacob B. Braddock, a rawboned countryman whose chin is fringed with white stubble, lived alone.

"This is old Christopher's Mills," he told us, just outside the old house, his piping voice shrill against the accompaniment of barking, provided by a vicious-looking dog. The animal was, Braddock admitted, "a bad one."

This farm was originally bought from the Indians, Braddock said, by one John Heulings. It was divided up into farms in 1775, from the original survey which covered about 40,000 acres. Once the property went over to Church Road and then to Jake Heulings' farm. John Christopher married one of John Heulings' two daughters and Amos Wilkins married Ann, the other. Braddock later married into the family and his farm today includes about two hundred acres.

The house, which has been rough-cast on one end, inconsiderately obscuring the date of construction, once served as a stopping point for weary travelers on the stage road. Here horses were fed and passengers stretched their legs. The other end of the house, perhaps the oldest part, is a tumbledown ruin.

There is little left of the mill. It was a sawmill, providing lumber and shingles for many of the dwellings long since dust. The mill was back of Braddock's farm, up Barton's Run. A few of its rotting boards jut out from the stagnant, wine-colored water below the sluiceway. Near by in the clearing, across from a cranberry storage house, there are papers left by picnickers. This is as far as many adventurers come. The bridge over which the stage road passes bears the dates 1830 and 1852.

From this point the road traverses through a hallway of pines and birches. There is a ditch of murky water running along at both sides, leaving the narrow, one-way wagon track on the ridge. The sides of the ditch and the edge of the woods have a carpet of yellow-green moss. For miles the traveling is through identical stretches. There are no houses. Only trees and swamps and tiny bridges, with the road turning but following in a general way, a straight line, convinces the invader that he is on an old abandoned artery of travel.

Pipers' Corner is the next name on the older maps. Here there are five points, the star-like intersection of many roads. One is the paved and much-traveled road to Atsion from Medford, on the line of old Shamong Township. Another trail breaks away to cross and recross the Indian Mills brook and later rejoin the main stem. Another, quite unintentionally, perhaps, leads to the new State road. Still another goes to Smalls, a tiny cluster of houses indeed, down from Flyat.

On the map it is Flyat. On the signposts, at least those

we saw, it is Flyatt. A strange name, either way you choose to spell it. Flyat is said to have been founded by three Revolutionary soldiers who became tired of fighting, deserted Washington and consequently changed their names.

Flyat is at the next cross of the Tuckerton Road. It is another of these crossroads of the pine country that will never need either a traffic light or policeman. Here, according to William Mackin, of Haddonfield, there was once a cluster of houses and a hotel. Mackin knew the Tuckerton Road well when a boy. There is now no dwelling of any sort at the intersection.

On what perhaps is the northwest corner there is a cow pasture inside a snake fence. Here there is an elevation on which the hotel must have stood. The hollow that was once a cellar has gradually filled in. Small cedar trees have grown among a few scattered bricks and beside a large stone that served once as a stepping-stone on which passengers of the coaches alighted.

If anyone recalls why the place was called Flyat, who flew and at what, we have never found them. Warner Hargrove, who knew nearly everything, like that at least, confessed the matter a puzzle to him.

Oriental is the next name on the map along the road, and then Hampton Gate. About where we judged Oriental to be, there is nothing to suggest the Far East. The owner of a large house at this crossroad informed us the intersection had become Naylor's Corner. Harvey Wells, the occupant, said this was once another stage stop.

"That's why the old barn's so close to the road," Wells loudly declared. "That was so the horses could be quickly unharnessed and changed while the riders stepped into the house for a bite to eat and something to drink." Prohibition habits compelled Wells to wink knowingly.

The road keeps on in much the same fashion: Bog and pine and sand and then pine again. There are one or two sawmills, their forgotten operations attested by stumps of cut pines and cedars. In one or two dips of the way, we detected the pungent smell of sawdust in the air, as well as the musical hum of saws. We saw little shed-like buildings surrounded by piles of carefully packed shingles and great logs standing ready as the raw material.

Hampton Gate, next on the road, soon proves that even the most alert wayfarer does not realize he is in town. Stopping at a tiny, unpainted house, in front of a more modern building, the Vineland Hunting Club, a middle-aged man with yellow teeth bared by a mechanical smile, appeared to answer our inquiries. He had not been the first, however, for a horse came galloping from the unfenced field, unmindful of the daring automobile we used.

"Is this Hampton Gate?" we asked. A child pressed a bright-eyed face against a plant-framed glass of the window.

"Part of it," said the man, making his way from the doorway with the aid of a stick. We did not ask where the rest of the town was for we had no cigarette to offer to stave off possible embarrassment. His trouble seemed to be rheumatism, a common malady among these folk who gain their living tending the berry bogs. This fellow's shoes were soggy and his thin trousers were wet to the knees.

We left the road and turned in along the Batsto River toward old Hampton Furnace. All the waters here are cranberry bogs, discarded berries forming a red ring along bays and coves when they are flooded. Finally after pass-

ing through woods and along picturesque lakes, one reaches
the home of David Kell, overseer of the Wilkerson and
Ryder bogs, well-known in this vicinity.

Kell is another rawboned individual, soft-spoken and retaining an accent peculiar to the folk of the pines. Kell
pointed out the site of the iron-smelting furnace of more
than a century ago, far across the clearing. The fields all
about are full of slag, the residue of the smelter's vanquished
trade.

"There was quite a town here once," Kell said. "Off
there in the clearing there were many houses. I can recall
a few of them rotting to pieces across the bog in the woods.
There was a cemetery, too, beside that buttonwood tree."

Here again the riddle of the world growing up and the
pinelands growing down, you see! Here there had been
an outpost of the great smelting industry, a village, families,
children. And now? Nothing at all, not even the cemetery. It once had wooden tombstones, Kell said, but they
are gone. Nothing but dry, waving yellow grass con-
fronted us. When the cranberry men came, Kell said there
was one house standing, but that was soon taken down.

The stream that runs to Batsto, the water of which operated the furnace itself, is clear as crystal. At its bottom
are some of the stones that tumbled from the furnace walls.
Down beside the bracken are charred timbers, the burned
remains of the old bridge and sluiceway, now replaced by a
modern concrete contrivance. In the thorny thicket is one
of the old furnace hammers, its head buried in the crum-
blings of long years, its handle protruding two feet from
the earth. It is a memorial nobody will pull out. Near-by,
close to the hidden fire-pits at which they worked, are rest-

ing the bones of an almost forgotten people of a long-forgotten town.

"You must grow lonely here," we said to Kell. "Cranberry season provides activity and interest, of course, but after all, that time is very short."

"Not at all," the overseer replied, "we're never lonely. There's always something to do. I'm used to it. You see, I've never lived any place mor'n nine miles from here."

"Gosh," one of us answered him, "don't you *ever* go anywhere else?"

"Sure," he replied. "Sometimes I go to Atsion and then sometimes, to Indian Mills. I generally get to one of 'em once a week."

Kell hasn't been to Camden in fifteen years!

But, come to think of it, who would worry about going to Camden?

Pine Grove Union Church, at the head of the old Tuckerton Stage Road near Medford.

Home of the hermit of La-Ha-Way, J. Turner Brakeley.

IX

THE HERMIT OF LA-HA-WAY

NORTHEAST of New Egypt and Prospertown, and not far to the east of the Ivanhoe Brook, there is a strange-named deserted village whose story struck us as decidedly unusual. Here, where older maps of the locality mark it down as the Lahaway Plantations and where those who know all about it call it "Layaway," is La-Ha-Way. The name is an Indian heirloom.

Taken from a tribe of Indians once making its headquarters in the locality, roaming the wilds of the Central Pines dividing the provinces of East and West Jersey, and making easy marches to the seashore for wampum, the name lingers on meaningless to many.

The Indians are mostly forgotten, except when relics are turned up in the woods and fields. However, two well-preserved dwellings, vacant, on the crest of a graceful knoll, remain to recall the memory of the strange man who spent his life in Lahaway in a voluntary exile.

The road to Lahaway is narrow and winding. Without a guide who knows his business you may miss it altogether. Charles Remine, of Wrightstown, took us there. Close by each side we saw a tangled mass fighting the invasion of an automobile. There was just room for a car to get through, cautiously, but the driver was ever on the alert for boggy ruts, fallen and broken limbs of trees, and possible traffic the other way. As on many such paths, one vehicle would be compelled courteously to back out of such a crisis.

Suddenly the pathway twists left through a cluster of pines and cedars. Through them, in passing, there is a glimpse of two more deserted buildings, weather-beaten and windowless. Then there is an unexpected halt for it is impossible to go any farther: The road, high on an embankment, attains an impasse where once there was a bridge. This has fallen among the charred timbers of a broken dam.

There is no need to ride on. From here the exploring is interesting on foot. On the hill are two painted and well-preserved houses, with barns behind them. Near them is a shaggy garden, blooming again, uncared for, unappreciated, contrasting the dried-up berry bogs across the way. There was a little pond where water lilies were to bloom, when we were there, and across it was a shaky, rustic bridge. This was Lahaway, the habitat of the Poet-Who-Never-Wrote-Verses.

In the legend of the countryside Lahaway and its poet-hermit are inseparable. The recluse was J. Turner Brakeley, remembered as a tall, well-built man with whitish hair and a well-trimmed beard. Born in Bordentown, Turner was the son of John Howell Brakeley, D. D., a Methodist preacher and proprietor of the defunct Bordentown Female College.

Brakeley, an only child, was well-educated. Aiming to prepare himself for a career at the Bar, he graduated from Princeton and later studied law at several other colleges. He was a personable, good-looking young man, devoted to his father, and unusually energetic. At twenty-five he seemed possessed of all that one could wish for.

It is with considerable reluctance that one makes public property the intimate details of Turner Brakeley's personal life, as gleaned from Remine, our guide, who knew the hermit well, as well as Mrs. Miller Emley, of New Egypt, widow of Brakeley's caretaker.

If the ghost of the poet should tap you on the shoulder at this precise moment and pointing to this account, say: "I only told that story once, so why should it be revealed after all these years?", the author, as well as the reader, would be decidedly at a loss for reply.

Since there is little likelihood of such a supernatural occurrence, since Brakeley's love affair was at the bottom of his exile at Lahaway, perhaps we can take a few liberties, being careful to write as sympathetically as possible. Surely, there have been a score of stories of what happened and if this one is true, as we have every reason to believe it is, some small service may be achieved in the task, even so.

Mrs. Emley did not know the name of the girl who changed everything in Brakeley's life, nor did she have any idea what became of her. Turner Brakeley spoke of her but once, and then, according to Mrs. Emley, talked quietly and mentioned no names. She was very beautiful, Brakeley said, recalling that they were betrothed. Apparently, he was to establish himself in the Law and then the wedding would be planned.

As Mrs. Emley recalls the story, the young woman was a student at the Bordentown College, the college directed by the hermit-to-be's father. Stories that Turner was jilted, as have been told from time to time, seem to be without foundation. Brakeley informed Mrs. Emley that it was he who broke the engagement. In the poet's brief, hesitating description of what happened, it came out that Brakeley unintentionally came upon the girl one evening in the arms of another man. He said he would not have seen the couple at all if it had not been for a sudden glance into a betraying mirror.

Apologies, explanations and pleas were to no avail. Turner Brakeley's dream had been forever shattered. It had been a vision of happiness so long in the making perhaps and here, in a moment, the possibilities of realization vanished forever. Whatever interpretation one puts on the incident, the story does not make Brakeley the unbending frump some of the legends persist in picturing him.

Turner went to his father with the disturbing announcement that he was going at once to live at Lahaway. He said that he wanted to be out of the sight of women and away from "the noise and bustle of the city." His father, the pastor, owned the land in and around the secluded spot and had built the dwellings that were there. Being interested in cranberry culture, Rev. John Brakeley had developed berry bogs where he found the plants already growing in wild profusion.

The minister received the news in astonishment. Here was his son, educated at considerable expense, on the threshold of a career and the more certain of success because of a comfortable legacy to which he had just fallen heir, telling him in a few terse sentences that he wanted nothing more than permission to take his few belongings and live alone in the heart of a desolate wilderness. Whether Turner went into details as to his reasons or whether his father remonstrated at any length with him, one can only surmise. At any rate Brakeley was soon established at Lahaway as a recluse.

From then on began the living of a strange and peculiar life almost entirely out of contact with the world and fellow-beings. To Lahaway, Brakeley brought enough furniture to make him fairly comfortable, some writing materials, ledger books, small plants and seeds, a supply of well-chosen clothing and odds and ends to make a home. He put people out of his mind. With a regular and ample income, he began at once to concern himself with the things he claimed to enjoy a great deal more.

First, Brakeley made the clearing larger. Then he planted many varieties of flowers throughout the vicinity. At long intervals he returned to civilization, but such visits were few. Back he would come with more clothing and more books, additional materials with which to study birds and bees and all Nature in this hermitage of his. Brakeley's study of wasps was more than ordinary. Pouring plaster into their earthen tunnels and digging out cross-sections, he demonstrated for his own satisfaction just how they lived. Several of these exhibits are on view in the collections at Princeton.

In one room in his house Brakeley placed five desks, arranging them in star fashion with a swivel-chair at the center. In these desks he filed away unlimited data on the winds and weather, the stars and the insects he observed so painstakingly. He read his barometer at eight each morning, at noon, at five each afternoon, and at midnight just before he went to bed. These notations were written down and filed away, day after day, with dates of bird arrivals, movements of the constellations, and the progress of new flowers.

Many old acquaintances recall when Brakeley arranged the little ponds in front of his home, cultivating lilies of many glorious colors to cover the surface of the water. These bloom on each year as his memorial.

Although Brakeley was mostly referred to as a poet, the title was given because of his appearance and habits. No

one seems to have ever known of his writing verse or anything more than the profusion of data which filled his desks
and his scattered boxes beside. Turner was a little difficult
to approach, Remine told us, but he was affable to those
who sympathetically visited the old plantation as long as
they didn't bother him too much or linger to stare or tres-
pass.

Early each morning the hermit would steal from the
house, Mrs. Emley remembers, and then sit atop "Cock
Robin Hill," as he called a near-by promontory. There he
would watch the sky and listen to the songs of the birds.

One legend has it that Brakeley brought the first carp to
this part of the State, carefully importing the fish from
Germany. During a storm, according to the story, his dam
broke and the progeny of the fish went swimming to several counties.

Another assertion is that the hermit made several invaluable corrective contributions to what had been known, up
to that time, of the habits of the wild duck and how the
fowl moved their young. Mrs. Emley recalls that Brakeley
used to tell of John Dove and his wife, only occupants of
Lahaway country at the time of his coming. It seems that
Dove shot a rabbit and brought it home for supper one afternoon and then, while he was in the woods, the tabbycat
subsequently devoured the rabbit. Unwilling to disappoint
her spouse, Mrs. Dove killed the cat, to obtain the bunny.
Her husband remarked, it was remembered, on the fine
flavor of the rabbit.

Brakeley showed unusual interest in the disappearance
of Old Black John, a colored peddler, who vanished in the
Ridge Woods back of Lahaway one day, to furnish another
unsolved mystery of the pinelands. No skeleton was ever

found but long, long after, in a high and sandy place, a hunter came across John's rusted and initialed snuffbox.

Mrs. Emley and her husband lived in the caretaker's house next door to the hermitage for fourteen years. Perhaps the most curious of her recollections reveals that Brakeley had his laundry done up only twice a year. He wore good clothing and was particular about his personal appearance and his food, but when he removed a shirt or a pair of trousers that had grown shabby, he tossed them into a storeroom until a six-months' collection had been gathered.

Of the hermit's death there are many uncertainties. It is known he was born January 10, 1847, and that he was photographed in September, 1908. These facts discredit the version that going to Lahaway when he was twenty-five he lived but thirty years thereafter. He died, as near as can be accurately learned, about 1912, in Bordentown. Relatives had removed him there when he was stricken ill.

The same kin, among whom there are names that must be carefully omitted, seemed unsympathetic toward Turner Brakeley's mode of living. With his death, members of the family visited Lahaway, and all its contents were ruthlessly destroyed. Most of the data was lost in the tirade, and so its real value is uncertain. Notes that had been taken for almost half a century were rooted out and thrown away. Jersey glass of untold value disappeared, old whisky was poured feverishly on the ground, and many Indian curios, meaningless except to the man who owned them, were hurled into the marshes where the poet's flowers still bloom in profusion.

And so Lahaway, or La-Ha-Way, as you may prefer to call it, remains today a game preserve, a clearing stretched

Forgotten Towns

vo houses whose rooms echo with an intruder's
s. There's old straw in the barns, rusted imple-
____ 1 the shed and murky water in the ice house, but
there is really nothing to recount the story of the hermit
whose hopes of happiness vanished with one brief glance
into a looking-glass.

The cranberry clearing, uncared for, bears no fruit.
Books and ledgers in which a poet wrote and wrote, to keep
himself from thinking, perhaps, have been dust long since.
Nothing, we were saying, remains to mark the passing of
this strange and lonely soul.

"Nothing?" queried his friend, Remine, reproaching us.
"Why, they've named a mosquito for him!"

And that, they assure us, is the case.

Ruins of the Ellis Adams farmhouse at Calico.

X

CALICO

Forsaken Calico, most elusive of the Lost Towns, was found only after many persistent expeditions.

Rising on an unexpected promontory from the cedar swamps, a lone chimney of Jersey stone stands sentinel in the midst of what was once a clearing and cultivated land. Beyond deserted cranberry bogs, two miles down a road impassable to everything but precarious foot travel, four miles northeast of deserted Martha Furnace—lies Calico.

Here within the past hundred years sheep have grazed. This chimney was a part of the cheerful fireplace of a farmhouse. Down the road were the homes of cranberry growers and families whose menfolk worked at the paper plant then in operation at Harrisville. Now all is silence, that weird stillness of the mucklands, the lifeless panorama on every hand that denies any semblance of a past.

Admission that after three years of searching, the Lost Town Hunters were about ready to admit failure in their quest of Calico, brought a most unusual response. Numerous telephone calls were received, as many letters came in and a number of those familiar with the exact whereabouts of the town reported in person to tell what they knew.

Hugh O'Neill, of Camden, reported that he had been born near Calico and had lived in a log cabin in Harrisville. He said he had left the pines when he was fourteen and though he was now sixty-seven, had never gone back. "And when we came to Camden and I saw brick houses and cobble streets for the first time, I wanted to go back to the pines right away," O'Neill declared. "I'd like to see the old place again—it must be changed by now."

Kirk Cramer, of Berlin, said that he had worked in the old plant at Harrisville where they made paper from marsh grass, and knew the road to Martha and Calico well. "My grandfather owned a farm there," he said, "and there my mother was born. She used to joke about how she made her first trip to Philadelphia on a load of iron ore and the excursion took three whole days."

Accompanied by O'Neill and Cramer, who, incidentally, met for the first time among the ruined walls of the Harrisville plant, years ago familiar to them both, we undertook what proved to be one of our most unusual ventures. To hear these men talk of old times in towns that have "grown down" while the world was growing up, was a treat by itself.

We ventured inland by way of Harrisia and Martha, through that long narrow pass that was a well-traveled road years ago. Bolstered by the firm assertions of our guides that we were on the right road and that Calico could not be far away, we parked our cars and walked on two miles further, picking our way through lowlands and on the tops of ruts in the submerged road. Gurgling rivulets were on all sides. The ground responded with a mushy sound at every step. Soon we came to a tiny bridge spanning a pool of cedar water, deep and clear.

"This," said Cramer, with authority, "is Beaver Run!" Looking up suddenly, he pointed ahead, crying out, "And there's my grandfather's house!"

The "house" was a lone chimney of Jersey ironstone.

When we saw it we knew we had been there before, that Calico had never been really lost to us. Several years ago, we had managed, somehow, to get a car through, after digging ourselves out of some of those blackish pools and from beside tiny bridges that broke through. They told us our pictures were of Munion Field. But this was Calico, after all!

Cramer's grandfather, who built the farmhouse that long ago fell in dilapidation and was swept by forest fires, was Ellis Adams. It was from this house that Cramer's mother made that memorable trip to Philadelphia, behind a six-mule team. Here there was a clearing of well-tilled soil. The Cramers have a bedspread, over 100 years old, made from wool of sheep raised at Calico.

"They combed the wool, spun it into yarn, dyed it themselves and—well, it is a product proving that Calico was really a town long ago," said Cramer. "George Mick lived over there across the road, with some of the Ryans. He was snitching pigs and horses from other residents from time to time."

"But nobody minded much," O'Neill put in. "They just gave him a haul-me-down and let it go at that."

We found the ruins of another house up another boggy road around the bend. Only a burned fence rail and a pile of broken bricks in the midst of a grassy plot show where one of the bog-tenders made a cozy home.

Cramer's mother was Ellen Adams. She married Charles B. Cramer of New Gretna. O'Neill's memories of Harrisville and Martha go back to when the former had a Main Street. Two men and nothing to do but keep it clean. "Remember Chris Hein, and—and Bill Holloway—and John

Harris?" he asked. "Why," Cramer replied, "I got my first pair of pants from that store in Harrisville. I remember, because my mother didn't like 'em."

The Harrisville store is now four bare walls in a charred barren village with a line of broken trees its only relics of Main Street days.

So intent on recollections and so keyed up by his return to the home of his ancestors was Cramer, that trudging on the way back he took a bad spill into the water covering the spongy road. We had to build a fire between the pools to dry out his clothing before we could return.

A mill grinder that belonged to Martha **Furnace**, one of the most important of the early bog iron works, built by Isaac Potts of Philadelphia in 1793.

XI

RATTLESNAKE ACE'S TOWN

To you for whom New Jersey is a map and its pinelands a picture of trees against the sky, Hanover Farms will be a commonplace name. Certainly there is nothing strange about it, like Ong's Hat, Double Trouble or Mount Misery. Although you will say that the name Hanover smacks of an overseas flavor, you will admit that the title is indicative of a realty development—Hanover Farms, lots on easy payments, attractive home sites for particular people, and all that sort of thing. But you would be wide of the mark.

The real estate of Hanover Farms, if it could be worthy of such reference, may have some value but nobody wants it. Someone has set its price, but who cares?

Geographically, Hanover Farms is located east of Mount Misery, south of Hanover Furnace and perhaps fifteen miles or so from Brown's Mills.

Of all the forgotten towns in the dense pine belt, Hanover Farms has perhaps had more chances to succeed than the others, with the possible exception of Whitings. Reading a time-table of the Pennsy for its line through Mt. Holly, from Camden to Toms River and Seaside Park, you will never find the name of Hanover Farms. You will, however, find the name of Upton—and that, as far as the pines are concerned, is the very same. For Hanover Farms is the town that couldn't make up its mind what it wanted to be called.

The railroad, for purposes of locating a station to whom

a passenger is an occasional intruder, bestowed a name of its own. We wondered, when we arrived there, if the place shouldn't have been called Hangover. Someone surely must have had a hangover, or perhaps the town is having one now.

In the last two decades, the jumping-off place has been variously known as Hanover, Hanover Station, Hanover Farms and Gravel Switch. The last name was the town's first. Some unimaginative person, observing that the soil was gravel and the station a siding on which could be loaded charcoal and wood, declared the title ought to advertise such remarkable characteristics.

Each of the names traced a new splurge of development. Old Hanover Furnace struck somebody as ideal for a resort and as the station was nearest, it took a relative name. When the wild project failed, the name faded as well. The railroad put up its box station and on it blazed the new and permanent name, Upton. Upton, a name the natives look at and pronounce Hanover even now.

There was purpose in the railroad's name. A millionaire, George B. Upton, of Boston, of whom mention was made at Mount Misery, came into possession of 25,000 acres of the lands near Hanover, and while booming the Farms with grave determination, made it, for a time, something of a shipping center.

Logs, pine boards, charcoal, cranberries, huckleberries and sand were sent into the world outside from this tiny station for a number of years. A few less than one hundred scattered homes sprang up, the Pineys grouped themselves for the organization of a town and New York promoters set men to work. The site of the village is much more accessible since the completion of the new roads.

In Hanover's heyday there was business, bustle and bonds. Investment securities were sold for various enterprises and the gullible fell prey to highly colored portraits of a new and promising town. The Hanover Farms Company handled the land. Business boomed with the establishment of such firms as the Brandiff Sand and Gravel Company, the Cement Product Company, the National Resources Development Company, the Bader Mill and Lumber Company, the Eureka Sand Company, and realty tracts known as Earlton Land Company, Brown's Mills Park, and Brown's Mills East.

The headquarters of all these concerns are now in ruins. Some, constructed of corrugated metal, are red with rust. Loose strips swing in the winds that sweep along the tracks. The various companies had brief uncertain history and then the long arm of the law closed their accounts. Many times receivers were appointed by the courts to sell the property at some sort of a price but the very best figure obtainable was four dollars an acre and this amount was not sufficient to pay accrued taxes and interest. Nobody, they told us, owns Hanover now and nobody cares a hang.

Boarding-houses, stores, mills, stables—all are prey to the elements. In this wraith of a village, however, there is still a population, even though it is less than half a dozen if you don't count snakes and deer.

There was the station master when we were there— since then he has been removed. Sometimes he was busy, he said. There were shipments of blueberries and cranberries to be attended to. Berries have short busy seasons, but a small portion of the year.

Finally, and most importantly, there is Asa Pittman.

Asa is more familiarly known to the wild countryside

as "Rattlesnake Ace." A son of the late Uncle Charlie Pittman who promoted Mount Misery, and a brother of Caddie Pittman, who with their mother, Aunt Sallie, lived on the Mount, Pittman is a native of the pines.

Don't get the idea that the few people of this land of unmistakable mystery dislike being alluded to as "Pineys." Most of them are rather proud of the distinction. And "Rattlesnake Ace" is more than proud of his forebears, his native heath and his little home near the station.

The Pittman house is a tiny dwelling, unpainted, set at the edge of the gray woods. Near it is an oil lamp on a pole, lit every night to show those who pass that somebody lives here. While trains whiz speedily by, Asa dwells here with his wife and small children, content with life and leisure.

A broad, large-boned man, with tawny skin and irregular teeth, he has recovered from a cancerous mouth which has twisted his weather-beaten face. In the deer season he serves as guide for hunters who go native for brief spells each year. At other times he earns his nickname by hunting and catching live pine and rattlesnakes. "Ace" sells them—in New York and sometimes other cities. They make shoes out of the skins of those the zoos won't take. Museums want them, mostly. Asa doesn't know and cares little what becomes of them. He catches them and ships them and collects his money. This is how the Pittman family ekes out its existence, "Ace" told us.

"Shore," said he, when we called on him. The sleet swirled down on the deer run out front where his Main Street was. "Here's one for you to see. But she's only a baby." He held up a live, wriggling rattler, three feet long and beautifully marked.

"Your sister, Cad, was telling us how she has to go out

and kill them to keep them away from the chickens," we recalled "You catch them instead, is that it?"

"Yep,"—with that toothless, chewing grin.

"How many snakes would you say you have caught?"

"Been catchin' 'em for twenty-five or thirty year."

"How many a year—one hundred?"

"More'n that."

"Two hundred?"

" 'Bout."

"Let's see," we told him, showing our prowess at figures, "that means you captured six thousand snakes!"

But that didn't seem a large figure to "Rattlesnake Ace."

"That makes you a sort of New Jersey St. Patrick," we suggested, but it is doubtful if Asa understood. He only grinned again.

The home of Rattlesnake Ace, Asa Pittman, at Hanover Farms-Upton.

The old mansion at Union Forge, where an Italian prince was born. The forge, a small one, made bar iron from ore hauled from Speedwell Furnace.

XII

PRESIDENT AND PRINCESS

THERE is nothing, surely, that bruises the heart as an old forgotten house does, a house that has been warm and carpeted and filled with the footfalls of those who have loved it, a house which, years after, is found cold, bleak, and forgotten.

There is such a house at old Union Forge, up the White Horse Road from Chatsworth. If walls could speak, these could tell a tale of glorious times, of royal and distinguished visitors from overseas, of days that followed the early and short-lived prosperity of the forge towns.

One more old house in the pinelands, you say, is nothing to get excited about. But this old place at Union Forge is really different. There is something in the atmosphere that hovers around it, something that makes you sure that here have passed grand personages. Even so, a great deal of Union Forge is mystery.

The house itself, from the outside, is hardly impressive. Its portico and a window here and there have been carelessly boarded up. Through the pines, not native trees, but species brought to the scene and planted, there glints the silver surface of little Lake Shamong, its lily-pads promising blooms to come.

Inside, there is something which at once moves you to pity, pity for any house, anywhere, that must be so deserted, so left the buffeting of elements knowing no reverence for tradition.

The first story they told us was that the mansion was once—and was still, as far as they could find out—the property of an Italian countess. Her name, they said, was Madame Talleyrand. We pointed out that if she were Italian she would have been a Signorina and, too, that the name, Talleyrand, sounded decidedly French.

It was then brought out that here in this very house a son was born to the wife of an Italian Minister to France, Rostollo by name. This dignitary who had served his Government more than twenty-five years ago, had returned to the Continent long since, but, it was said, the boy who was born here in the pines was expected to return some day to the old, dark house. Jonathan Godfrey, who represented the estate and affairs of the family, was expected to sail for Paris, to return, ultimately, with the young Rostollo.

Our investigation failed to reveal, however, any Minister with a name exactly like the one given us and it may be that the miles and years that lie between this legend and the heydays of old Union Forge have allowed unintentional discrepancies. According to records, a Prince Mario Ruspoli de Toggio-Suisa was first secretary of the Belgian Embassy from Italy in those forgotten years, serving until 1910. It may be that the name should be Ruspoli, rather than Rostollo, and it may be, as the natives say, that the young prince intends doing something for the house in which he was born.

Entrance is gained through a side door that bangs dismally when the winds are up. Almost immediately one is in an awesome reception hall. Here is a tremendous mid-Victorian fireplace and a wide stairway, marred by a broken balustrade. Over the floor, in fact on the floor of every room in the house, there is a soft, dusty deposit of dried moss, gathered by someone who intended to dry it out for a florist, and then forgot.

The mental processes of certain peculiar people in this world will never be quite understood. Among such are those miscreants who, apparently unable to find a deer or smaller quarry in the woods outside, fired quantities of buckshot into the base of the tall scrolled pillars at the foot of the stairs, battering bricks from the fireplace itself.

The sunlight streams through the broken windows of the veranda, seeking to dry the moldy mass upon the floor as well as the soggy red silk which once covered the walls, and now hangs in strips from the ornate molding. The banister from the second-floor hall has been hurled over on the steps by another of those idiotic marauders who have picnicked here.

The rooms upstairs which once had charm have lost in bare walls all but their memories, tattered recollections of days when gay-gowned women passed through them, primping for the dance whose music echoed from below. The fireplace, beside which a royal mother may have crooned in the flickering shadows thrown from a great fire, is but a crumbling black hole. Such reflections are usually rudely ended by the patter of footsteps on the rotting roof as a squirrel seeks his hiding-place.

There is a ruin of a building out front offering plausible explanation of these legends and providing a historic background for this lavender and old lace. This was once a large clubhouse, located directly across the road from the furnace site. That the place was an imposing structure is shown by the two huge chimneys which point to the sky from a heap of broken lumber and piles of crumbled brick.

The club was erected about 1890 by a group of New

York capitalists, headed by Levi P. Morton, Vice President of the United States from 1889 to 1893. Morton was primarily a banker and had been head of the L. P. Morton Co., of New York, which had an influential London branch. Levi Parsons Morton, born in Shoreham, Vermont, in 1824, had figured prominently in the Alabama Claims Case against Great Britain and had succeeded in collecting $15,-500,000. In 1895 he became Governor of New York, his death concluding an eventful life on May 16, 1920, at Rhinebeck.

The secrets of the mysterious princess's house were spun, most likely, in days that followed Morton's service as Minister to France, from 1881 to 1885. He brought many of his European friends to this country and surely the damsel may have been among them. Here in Southern New Jersey, at Chatsworth, a gunner's town, was forged a lasting link of international friendship. One can picture the club, far enough off from the cities to prevent "nosey" gossip-mongers from prying and near enough to observe an engagement schedule.

Money was spent like water in advertising the club, they told us. The financiers sought to interest dignitaries of the Victorian days in a sequestered hide-out where they could spend a quiet week-end with anyone they chose and with no one the wiser. But the scheme failed, even though there were no columnists or tabloids operating then.

Finally, the story goes, with the building heavily in debt, it was discovered afire one night and its insurance money was said to have repaid partially those who had invested in it.

Of the old forge, little at all is evident. Down in the undergrowth at the other side of the roadway is a pile of slag,

just as at old Hanover and Speedwell. Union Forge, as a
smelter's town, is a memory more dim than that of Martha,
Lebanon, or Washington.

Union Forge is part of old Woodland township, which
has a total of 73,459 acres. This vast area, until a short time
ago, showed a total of only eighty scattered voters. The
real power of the township is Willis Buzby, "King of the
Pineys," who with his son, Jack, operates a combination
store, service station and garage in Chatsworth. Willis,
with his ready advice on law, etiquette, investments, medicine and religion, will tell you the story of Union Forge
much better than it has been recorded here.

Chatsworth is a town of the present but only the past
has atmosphere, atmosphere that clings to that old deserted
house on the White Horse road. Some moonlight night we
plan to go back and listen to the Pineys singing the official
Chatsworth Song, beside the shore of Lake Shamong:

> "In Shamong they grow pertaters,
> And they grow 'em small—
> They eat 'em hides and all—
> In Shamong!"

Arched oven of the Pasadena Terra Cotta Company, destroyed by fire in the early 1900's. In the left foreground is a trap door, one of the many through which the unwary may drop to hidden underground kilns.

XIII

PASADENA, NOT CALIFORNIA

THERE are people in Southern New Jersey who still believe that the earth is not round at all, but rather, that it has the shape of an egg.

Preposterous, you say—but it is not. Listen to the story of Pasadena, a deserted hamlet across the Ocean County line, nearer Whiting than Chatsworth, but on the Jersey Central, trail of the fast Blue Comet. Pasadena's modern name is Wheatlands.

Perhaps no one there ever came into the open with the baldly expressed theory that the world is like an egg, but many have definitely held that at Pasadena the center of the earth is close to the surface, and that there is but a few feet of "crust" between them and the torrid middle of the universe.

What there is or ever was at Pasadena to give life to such a belief has no existence now except in the legends that linger with memories of a village of scattered gun clubs that no longer deserves a name.

There is, of course, the story of Peggy Clevenger and her husband, Bill. They told us there that Bill, who died in 1872, lived what was said to be a far from sanctimonious life in and about old Pasadena. Before dying, he told Peggy that if he found conditions of the next world as they had been described to him, strange things would soon happen close to home.

Bill assured Peggy that if his new stamping ground was

as hot as he had been led to believe, he would cause the water of an open well near their house to boil day and night. The legend recounts that on the night after Bill passed on, the water in the well began to bubble and steam, sure enough.

The well no longer exists. Its walls long ago caved in and the place where it once was has been forgotten. One old resident of Pasadena was careful to emphasize the fact that the story was not all fable. Henry Webb swore to us that he saw the well. Henry said it continued to boil, now and then, until its walls crumbled.

Peggy is well remembered, too. Despite the fact that she lived back in the pines, far beyond the Plains, she was a fairly wealthy woman. Her mistake was in an unholy joy with which she showed all who plunged through to the little hamlet a stocking filled with gold which soon became the envy of the whole community.

One dark and chilly night, not long after Bill's death, Peggy's house, a ramshackle structure, burned to the ground, the old woman dying horribly in the flames. Though the ruins revealed what had been her body, no trace was ever found of the hoarded money and it was generally conceded, for many years, that Peggy had been robbed, murdered, and burned to conceal the crime.

There is something in the soil of the acres around Pasadena which gives it a springy, spongy quality, although it appears to be mostly like sand. There is a queer something giving the earth a hollow sound. It is as if one were walking on an earth-covered roof of some subterranean passage.

At Pasadena, the crazy legend of the earth's heat seems to have been reflected in many unforgettable tragedies of fire. In the recollection of the few present inhabitants not less than five small houses have burned, taking with them one, and in some cases, more than one life. Perhaps old Bill Clevenger put a curse on the town after his wife was so cruelly trapped in her shack.

The final fire was disastrous and it swept the lone factory venture, the Pasadena Terra Cotta Company, out of existence. This concern was a plant of considerable size, judging by its tumbled ruins, and it manufactured pottery and terra cotta materials. It was destroyed in the early 1900s, they told us.

Over the old ovens the vines have woven a mantle of green. Lizards scramble from niches in the broken masonry. The plant itself, whose history seems a little obscure, is by no means as old as Pasadena, but its dreams are in the same oblivion to which the village is fast moving downhill.

There are twisted rails along which ran the donkey engines to and from the clay pits. Charred boards and ties tell the story of the fire. Through the clearing, strewn with clusters of prickly pears, cactus of the pine belt, there are footprints of deer and queer trapdoors through which one may fall to the deserted underground bins.

Rusted rails lead to where a break in the trees is glimpsed across the hill. Near Woodmansie, two engines, boarded up and abandoned where they stood the morning after the fire, have since been removed.

The story of Pasadena would be but half told if we did not make some mention of Billy Bryan's place. Billy had his best years during the times of the Great Commoner's ascendancy. Billy, his namesake, enjoyed playing host at his substantial home to friends from Pennsylvania and all parts of New Jersey. When Billy was not in Wheatlands, he could be located at Green's Hotel, in Philadelphia.

Billy and his friends were the center of colorful gatherings and escapades of the old town. These events took place, mostly, at Gallagher's Spring, an obscure hide-out back in a cedar swamp. The secret of the spring and its lodestone powers was not a magic water, or even a liquid that bubbled and smoked, as in the Clevenger well, but a rare assortment of old wines and liquors, cool, enervating, and refreshing.

Warner Hargrove recalled visiting the place, years ago. It was about a half mile from any building in Pasadena, he said, and was a spot difficult to attain. When one reached it, however, the world and its troubles were entirely forgotten for at least a little while.

After the pottery plant was abandoned, a fruit farm of considerable size was begun and had some success. This farm was in operation until recently, utilizing the Central for shipments. Agriculture of any sort is hampered hereabouts, however, by deer that wander through the pines. This is the heart of the deer country. Here among the stories of old towns, Red Oak Grove, Half Way, Webb's Mill, Aserdaten and Bullocks, these graceful creatures, bred from the State game farm at Forked River, wander in contentment on all but five days of the year.

From Pasadena, it is necessary to go twelve miles for a postage stamp. Roads are winding sand trails that all but vanish as they meander through the scrub or follow parallel to the railroad tracks as if for safety's sake.

This is Pasadena, a libel on its California namesake.

XIV

SMITHVILLE—HIGH-BICYCLE TOWN

ON MARCH 6, 1850, the New Jersey Legislature set apart Westhampton Township in Burlington County, and pointed out, among boundary points, Cox's Landing or Lane Road, Timbuctoo, Unionville, Smithville and Turpentine.

Cox's Landing, Lane Road, Timbuctoo, and the settlement of Turpentine, appearing in the vicinity of Mt. Holly on the older maps, have now disappeared. Leaving the pine country for an interval, it might be appropriate to talk about old Smithville, South Jersey's high-bicycle town. Smithville, be it understood, is not a forgotten village in the ordinary sense of the word. But its heydays, days of the world's only bicycle railroad, days when the automobile was an entertaining but fantastic dream, are seldom recalled.

Smithville lies twenty miles from Camden and somewhat farther from Trenton. It is on a back road but its appointments are as good as many better-situated villages of the same size enjoy throughout the county. Here amid the relics of old times, heirs to traditions of its founder and the men who once rallied around him, Smithville continues to operate the machine company which once made it world-famous, turning out all sorts of wood-working apparatus for present-day use.

When Hezekiah B. Smith, Smithville's founder, came to New Jersey, his arrival was the climax of an already active career. Born in Bridgewater, Vermont, in 1816, he had developed the making of furniture by hand and then had worked out machinery to achieve the same purpose. Despite various discouraging setbacks, success came at the early age of thirty-one.

At this time Smith located at Lowell, Massachusetts, and his business grew to large proportions. When it became evident that further expansion would be necessary, Smith came to Southern New Jersey and was pleased with a little village he found near Mt. Holly, then called Shreveville, sometimes Shreveport. Here two brothers named Shreve operated a water-power mill beside the Rancocas creek.

The Shreves had several serviceable large buildings, somewhat out of repair. The water power was a deciding asset, something to offset the frowns that followed first appraisals of the dilapidated manor house and untenantable buildings near it. The only prosperous place in town was an old inn where liquor was sold in great quantity.

A little archaic in its appearance, the town nestled in a valley that followed the creek, as distinctively individual in character as though hundreds of miles separated it from its nearest neighbor. Smith, young and ambitious, visioned a town that would resemble a Guild village of the Old World, where each citizen could be a master-craftsman with a heritage of mechanical skill handed down from father to son. Smith bought the town, just as it stood.

The purchase included about 2000 acres of land in and surrounding Shreveport. Upon his permanent arrival, Smith made an arrangement with postal authorities and the railroad company operating on a single track, to change at once the name of the town and station. With the Shreves moving out, he said, there could be no Shreveport. With the Smiths moving in, Smithville must be definitely established. And Smithville it has remained for almost one hundred years, quaint, peaceful, and unhurried, fostering a spirit of progress in manufacture, and forever attesting the ingenuity and inventive genius of three generations of Smiths.

First there was old Hezekiah, then his son, Elton A. Smith, and later his sons, Allen and Earle, who continued to operate the machine company carrying on the town's traditions.

When Smith took possession of the property, everything was changed. The treadmills became machine shops, new buildings rose from ruins, foundries and smithies were built and new water wheels, with castings of iron and masonry that will stand for years to come, supplanted the antiquated ones. The mansion house was repaired, rebuilt and given additions. Billiard rooms, bowling alleys and brick stables were erected. Parks were laid out for the breeding of rare animals. Greenhouses and conservatories were provided for imported tropical plants.

In the process of building and rebuilding, Smith took away the saloon and a large fireproof house was constructed for the convenience of workmen who would have to board. A building for theatricals and meetings was placed in the center of the new town. Reading rooms were appointed, invested with books, and little farms were mapped out and planted. Then, with the job finished, Hezekiah Smith looked proudly over his domain, his town. The machine shops were put into operation.

The plant shortly after was incorporated as the H. B. Smith Machine Company and as such soon became famous for the manufacture of woodworking machinery. Everything was still humming merrily when, about 1880, the bicycle craze hit the country. Smith saw what was coming and made ready. Machinery, building machinery, was soon put to turning out the famous "Star" bicycle.

The "Star" had two wheels, with the small one, twenty inches in diameter, in front; and the large one, having a diameter of thirty-nine inches, behind. The contraption stood high, and was guided by the smaller front wheel. Both wheels had solid rubber tires similar to the horse-drawn vehicles of the day. A frame, from the hub of the back wheel to the top of the front, supported the saddle and handlebars. The rider, taking a running start, towing the machine from a small step on the frame, finally mounted—after due practice, of course.

This new means of transportation was novel as well as "speedy." One had to go quite fast, first of all, to keep the bicycle upright. Naturally too, gravel or smooth-surfaced roads were best for riding since cobbles caused many a disaster or at least a rough ride on solid tires. "Stars" were being ridden in all sections of the country in no time, and to-day one of the early models occupies a place in the transportation division of the Smithsonian Institution, next to the early models of the Haynes and Ford automobiles.

George W. Pressey, inventor of the bicycle, made the model of the first "Star." As the up-to-date advertising feature for the unprecedented Smithville vehicle, Thomas Finley, then a well-known athlete, was employed to make a tour of nearby States on the new bike. In Washington, to show what the new wonder of wonders could do, Finley told the world that on a certain day and at a certain time he would ride bravely down the Capitol steps.

Police were on hand as a result and Finley was arrested

and put in jail just as he poised his "Star" ready for the ride. Later, paying his fine and obtaining his release, he secured sufficient "pull" to persuade officials that the feat would not be too hazardous. Finley's ride down the steps, accomplished without mishap in the presence of many old-time newspaper writers, won nation-wide notoriety.

Finley until recently lived in Mt. Holly, amused by recollections of his athletic days. Once he appeared with his bicycle at the Academy of Music in Philadelphia as a special attraction on a program with James Whitcomb Riley. On another occasion he rode the slopes of Mt. Washington, he told us, perilously poised on a "Star." He laughed at the marvels of his youth, when he spoke of automobiles, flashy, silent-engined and streamlined, passing by his home at high speed.

The story goes that a pneumatic tire was invented in Smithville, by an employe of the plant, William S. Kelly. But Kelly, who died several years ago, never reaped any benefit from his device, they told us, because he did not realize its importance until too late.

Smith was never content to march with the main procession. He was always thinking ahead, working out what tomorrow's demands might be. One unusual tale they tell at Smithville concerns its founder's own automobile adventure. That was back in 1879, long before Henry Ford was tinkering on his first model.

The Smithville plant seems to have turned out a sure-enough automobile, a steamer with a kerosene-burning, sixteen-inch fire-tube boiler, a three-speed sliding gear and a high-speed, piston-valve motor. The strange thing about it is, according to the story, that the machine worked amazingly well.

Hezekiah Smith realized, however, that if the world was still a little skeptical of the bicycle it surely wasn't ready for the automobile. So, with his customary decision, he concluded the trial run with a mechanic, saying, deliberately: "Fritzie, take it back to the barn. We're twenty years ahead of the times!"

Then came the "bicycle railroad." This specialty was devised, first of all, for the use of employes of the Smith plant who came to work from Mt. Holly. The only other means of transportation besides shank's mare was a slow train or horse-and-buggy. The depots for the trains were then a long distance from residential sections. So the bike railroad was conceived and constructed, operating from Mt. Holly to the very center of Smithville.

Substantial posts were set in the ground to a height of about four feet. On these posts were fastened a wooden "stringer." On its top was a grooved metal rail of special design. This was all the track needed except at each terminal, where there were a number of switches. The bikes themselves were constructed to accommodate from one to four passengers who rode much as they did on horseback, the propelling power being supplied by pedals as in the principle of the "Star."

Clarence Hotchkiss, inventor of the railroad, thought at first that his idea would have world fame. As far as is known, however, the line was never duplicated anywhere else. Beginning operation about 1895 it fell into disuse when old Hezekiah died.

With the successful operation of the machine shops, old "H. B.," as he was affectionately known, became more than a local figure. In his later years he took an unusual interest in politics and was elected to Congress, where he

The monorail bicycle railroad invented and built by Hezekiah B. Smith to carry employees from Mt. Holly to his bicycle plant in Smithville.

The Anniversary of the Battle of New Orleans.

1815.

1880.

ANDREW JACKSON

Grand Ball at Smithville, N. J., Jan. 8, 1880.

LADIES INVITATION.

One of the most colorful of New Jersey's forgotten towns, Smithville in its heyday had a gaming casino and an elaborate opera house and ballroom. The Smithville Brass Band was famous all over the state.

Hezekiah B. Smith and his bicycle railroad.

An early Star model featured a ratchet-drive mechanism.

served on several important committees, notably on one which supervised the granting of patents. He introduced a measure for the publication of complete reports of patented inventions so that inventors would not be long in finding the information they sought. Later he became State Senator and could have returned on the expiration of his term but he withdrew from the active field.

Smith to the last devoted himself to his namesake town. Among his workmen he organized and developed a band of good size and ability. The band, if you please, attained so much fame that it once performed at the historic Philadelphia Academy of Music. When Smith campaigned for political office he took his band with him. A staunch Democrat, he celebrated his many elections with great jollifications to which members of all factions and parties were invited. Ox-roasts, barbecues, and the wassail bowl of such affairs are among the mellowest memories of old Smithville.

Old Hezekiah was very fond of music. It is said that often when he went to his lawn to read he engaged some musician from among his men to play the violin somewhere near by. When he died, his band played a funeral march for the cortège, through his own prearrangement.

Another strange memory of old Smithville, as it used to be, is that of Hezekiah's trained moose. He purchased it and had it harness-broken. Afterward, to the amusement of the pedestrians and discomfiture of horse-owners, "H. B." used to drive his moose down the road, chasing everything to cover. Horses shied and hauled carryalls into miry ditches. Riders, perched on their high bicycles, dodged up side lanes whenever the moose claimed the road.

When Hezekiah died and was buried to accompaniment

of mournful strains from his band, Smithville was tied up in a brisk legal battle that attracted interest for many years. The fate of the town was uncertain for a long time in the contest over the estate.

Smith had lived in Lowell, Massachusetts, and there had married. From this union there had been one son, Elton. When Elton reached maturity, he established himself in Savannah, Georgia, and his mother went to live there with him. It may have been that Mrs. Smith didn't care for these town-founding and machine-inventing plans of her husband. During all the years when Hezekiah was establishing his pioneer woodwork machinery plant and village, his wife remained in the South.

During this time a well-known actress, Agnes Gilkenson, came into the picture mysteriously. There are many stories of how Agnes established herself in the Smithville mansion but all are fringed with improbability and conjecture. During her reign, however, there was imported from Italy a beautiful statue, a likeness of herself, a really charming figure that was placed on the sloping lawn overlooking the lake. When Hezekiah died, the widow and her son returned and smashing the statue in many pieces, hurled it forever to the bottom of the pond.

Smith provided in his will for the establishment of a vocational school, providing one of the earliest documents in which mention of such a project is recorded. After a fight of ten long years, fraught with many legal skirmishes and return fire, Mrs. Smith and her son, Elton, succeeded in breaking the testament, the courts finally acknowledging the rights of the widow and her son. The factory has been carried on ever since.

Hezekiah, during his day, surrounded himself with loyal

men who built the foundation for a lasting reputation. Kelly, the tire inventor; George Lippincott, and Charles S. Brown were among these. But with the death of "H. B." there was a change. The band was given up, the rare animals were disposed of and the plants and flowers in the conservatories were abandoned.

Log house with frame addition in what was Stockingtown, named for a hosier who didn't believe in signs. He merely hung a stocking on the end of a pole.

Barnegat Light as it looked a quarter of a century ago.

XV

WARETOWN AND THE QUAKER BAPTISTS

DOWN where a brisk breeze ever sweeps across the bay, off the Jolly Tar Trail a little to the northwest of Barnegat, is a cluster of homes. There are less than fifty of them, a store, a couple of churches and a Post Office. An inscription on a garage that has certainly seen better days and a signboard over the Post Office door announce the place as Waretown.

Isolated because modern progress has taken the New York-Atlantic City highway further inland, Waretown strings along a mile or so on a crescent-shaped spur which two hundred years ago was part of the only seashore highway. Here where the world and a handful of its people take their time together once lived the originals of that most peculiar of sects in the Colonies, the Rogerine Baptists.

In Ocean County where winter's enforced peace and daydreaming contrast summer's bustling excursionists and holiday-seekers, distant descendants of Quaker Baptists remain. Out on the hill that slopes to the bay, in a grove of plume-like cedars, sleep the leaders of this queer and forgotten clan.

It was in 1737 that a group of the original Rogerines established themselves in Waretown, which, in that day, was spelled Waeirtown. Abraham Waeir, it is supposed, founded the village some time before and when exponents of the new faith moved in, allowed himself to be converted.

Years later, after most of the Quaker Baptists had moved back to their former haunts in North Jersey, Abraham stayed on guard in the town that bore his name.

The society of the Rogerine Baptists was founded about 1674 by John Rogers, a zealous man with some very original though clean-cut ideas of religion. He and his followers believed in baptism by immersion, the celebration of the Lord's Supper in the evening with ancient and forgotten appendages, and the observation of every day in the week as a holy day.

To the followers of Rogers, the Sabbath held no special sanctity. They held that since the death of Christ all days had become holy alike. They scorned the use of medicines and tonic herbs, employing neither physicans nor surgeons. They refused to say grace at meals and insisted that all prayer, except that inspired by extreme occasions, must be offered mentally.

As Quaker Baptists, this group, whose pioneers became some of Waeirtown's first residents, declared that all unscriptural parts of religious ritual were idolatry. All good Christians, they said, should exert themselves against idols. Infant baptism and observance of Sunday were idolcraft and the Sabbath was a New England idol to be shunned.

The Rogerines were not content with practising their religious belief off by themselves and undisturbed in the new land of religious freedom. They insisted on enforcing their ideas on their neighbors to the disturbance of other churches. It is recorded that they went to meeting houses and other buildings where divine services were being held, deliberately making a show of manual labor. The women would knit in their pews and the men would whittle, every now and then bursting out with contradiction of the preachers.

A little of this sort of thing went a long way. If the Rogerines were seeking persecution, they got it. New Englanders left some of them neither liberty, property nor whole skins in any number of cases. However, here on the Bay of Barnegat the trouble-makers may have caused scenes, but in Waeirtown, at least, they seem to have escaped serious consequences of such conduct.

John Rogers, founder of the sect, was a churlish and contrary fellow. For more than forty years he preached his strange ideas and died a death in 1721 that contradicted them. With smallpox raging in Boston, Rogers disregarded all warnings and boldly journeyed to the stricken city in order to put his beliefs to the test. He was fully confident that his faith would guard him from the dread disease. Poor John not only was stricken by contagion but communicated it to his family and neighbors before he himself expired. His followers carried on.

A company of Rogerines was set upon in Norwich, Conn., in 1725, for making a disturbance on the Sabbath. The group was unmercifully beaten and finally driven from the Colony. Whereupon Governor Jenks, of Rhode Island, who wanted to say something appropriate as they passed through to swell the Jersey clan, wrote spiritedly against their cavortings and assailed them as inciters of riot.

In the Norwich group was a family named Colner. John Colner, his wife and their five sons and five daughters, moved to New Jersey in 1734. They first made their abode on the east side of Schooley's Mountain in what is now Morris County. But this section did not suit them very well, and they went on down to Waretown, which was then in Monmouth County. Here they held their meetings in a schoolhouse and made but few attempts to interrupt the devotion of more pious people.

The wandering Rogerines spent about eleven years in Waretown and then shifted headquarters back to North Jersey. But they left behind them a group of persons who had been touched by their teachings and who continued to practise their beliefs without a leader. By 1790, however, there were but two known Quaker Baptists left, Thomas Colner and Sara Mann.

In Waretown, despite the years that have passed and the changes that have come, they tell an unusual story of a Rogerine couple. The Rogerines believed that marriages need not be performed, that a man and woman could marry in theory without the restraint of any ceremonial vows. Accordingly, a man and woman, following the show-off ways of their beliefs, presented themselves to the Governor, tantalizing him with the assertion that they had "married themselves" without benefit or consent of Church or State.

The Governor frowned a moment and then said, "What! Do you take this woman for your wife?"

"Yes, I most certainly do!" replied the man.

"And do you take this man for your husband?" pursued the Governor, sharply addressing the woman.

"Of course," she declared.

"Then," replied the wily old executive with a smile, "in the name of the Commonwealth I pronounce you husband and wife. Whom God hath joined together let no man put asunder." The couple retired, much chagrined.

A little white church, said to be on the foundations of

the school used by the Rogerines, is still standing. It was used later by a company of Universalists but has not been in service for more than twenty years. Inside, intact, are old-fashioned pews, a small pulpit, the organ, old hymn books and oil lamps.

All but hidden off the main road, Waretown is different today. In the Post Office they sell groceries, candy and pastry. When we walked in to ask a few more questions, a produce man was there buying "a nickel's worth of this" and a "nickel's worth of that" of the postmistress. Finally he was sauntering out.

"Don't want any lemons?" he asked, hopefully.

"No," replied the woman, and then, "well, you might bring me three."

"Couldn't use a dozen?" asked the man in a drawl.

"No," definitely. "I don't want to sell them. Just use them myself."

There, in a few words, you have the spirit of Waretown!

The Methodist meetinghouse at Port Elizabeth, erected in 1827. The original church, a frame structure, was built in 1786.

The dance pavilion at Brindle Town, where Burlington County's master-detective, Ellis Parker, fiddled on Saturday nights in the 1890's.

XVI

BRINDLE TOWN

ON THE edge of the pinelands in Burlington County, five or six miles east of Wrightstown and south of New Egypt, there is a forgotten village known as Brindle Town.

Nobody lives at Brindle Town now to remember how it got its strange name. Brindle, says the dictionary, is a streaking of color—but all color is gone from this deserted village. Former days were colorful, perhaps, but the present is one with that mysterious, unfathomable, uncanny atmosphere that palls on the whispering pines.

Brindle Town, if it still cares to boast of a name, has become the more impressive Brindle Park. Somebody may have considered that there is more park than town in this village where, not so long ago, there echoed the joyous shouts of boys who enjoyed the first Ockanickon Camp.

We found Brindle Town on a sandy, muddy road out of Cookstown. The road became a trail and the trail a cow path long before we attained our destination. Then, abruptly at the end of the single telephone line, there is a little group of untenanted buildings.

One, largest of all, is painted. Its shutters clatter in the wind and through the rooms the breeze sweeps last Autumn's leaves across the floor. Some of the windows are broken. Through others a trespassing gunner has drilled many holes with small caliber bullets. Inside, the dwelling is damp and dark.

This was the hotel, scene of gay times in sprightlier days.

All of Brindle Town was owned then by John G. Hutchinson and later by the heir of his estate. The Hutchinson holdings included about one thousand acres, one third of which was the lake. Brindle Lake is one of the most picturesque in this portion of New Jersey and the hotel, headquarters of the Hutchinsons long ago, looks out upon it from a wide, sloping unkempt lawn.

From among untended flower beds, squirrels scamper at intruding humans, over the dried grass, up the posts of the portico and across the roof with lightning speed, scurrying into the hotel garret through a break in the rotting shingles. The merry travelers are gone. No more will rooms be let, as in the lively days, at five dollars a week, no more whisky will be sold at five cents a glass, no matter what the times are.

Not far away there is a deserted tumble-down shed, while out along the shore of the lake are decaying boathouses, unused and unvisited. Under them the waters of the lake lap in monotonous tattoo. Behind the dam, repaired against more ravages of the spring and summer rains, is a frame-like building that was once a mill and later served as the dining hall for one of the earliest Y.M.C.A. camps. To gain an entry here is now impossible: the boardwalk has tumbled away and the mill, a hollow shell, stands high as if on stilts.

Back from the mill at the edge of the dismal, repellent swampland, across from the hotel itself, is a well-made building, perhaps in the best condition of all. This was the dance hall, where folk from four counties once gathered for jamborees. Inside, along all four walls is a continuous rude wooden bench on which the spectators were wont to sit so as to watch the fun. There is a special niche for an orchestra.

It was here that Ellis Parker, before his rise to national prominence as a detective, was the town's official musician.

Ellis was a fiddler, back in 1889, serving as one-third of the Brindle Town orchestra from 1889 to 1897. Ellis bowed a fiddle, Joe Raymond strummed an auto-harp and Jake Walker plucked a banjo.

The premises of Brindle Town were available in those days for picnics at all times except Sundays and Mondays. No activities of any kind were permitted on those days, the property being reserved for the owners and their more intimate friends, the Newbolds, Bishops, Bryans, Blacks, and Bullocks. On other days anybody could have a free and easy time and many did, eating supper, tuning up on cheap but potent liquor, and then going in for the dance.

Chief Parker was then eighteen and one of the best fiddlers in the pine country. When he started jig tunes to the accompaniment of Joe and Jake, heels began to shuffle in old square dances, the quadrille, the polka and all the rest.

Ellis and his musicians in those days each charged five dollars. At times Chief Parker would conduct the dance himself, charging a fee of "five cents per corner" when square dances were in vogue. Payment was for the most part in silver but very often Ellis accepted five and ten cent cranberry tickets given as a scrip salary at the well-known bogs of Empson, Tantum, and Brakeley.

Although Detective Parker had not as yet dreamed of adventures as a Hawkshaw, he was a firm believer in law and order. At his dances he posted notices to the effect that fights would not be permitted on the dance floor. Scrappers were required to battle it out at least one hundred feet from the dance pavilion. Nobody broke the rules, Ellis told us, when we described our visit to Brindle Town.

There was a Farmer's Day once a month. Musicians would be imported to enlarge the orchestra from Wrightstown and Pointville. Brindle Town was a beehive of action then, picnickers sprawling on the lawns and cooking in the woods, fishermen casting for trout in the lake, and thirsty roisterers singing lustily on the hotel portico.

That Chief Parker chose a life of criminal detection rather than music was due, he told us, to merest chance. A horse belonging to his father was stolen. Ellis appointed himself a committee of one to find out who stole it. He located the horse and the thief as well, making so much of an impression that the old Burlington County Pursuing and Detecting Association took notice.

This organization had been formed during Civil War times to protect the New Jersey farmers from raiding horse thieves. When Parker duplicated his achievements in several auspicious instances, he was engaged by the Pursuing Society to take on specific assignments. From then on, criminal investigation became his life work. Today he is unquestionably the most famous murder authority in the East.

The society for which he started work kept up its activities until a few years ago when the advent and the development of the automobile crowded horses out of the picture, and there were few horse thieves to hunt down. The organization disbanded.

Campers and picnickers still go to Brindle Town. Just now, however, all is silence and desolation.

There was one thing puzzling about the first trip we

made there, however. Somebody, surely a woman, had been walking up and down every path in sight. The mark of French heels was plain in the sand, over the spillway and around the old hotel. There were no other footprints. We told Ellis Parker he ought to explain the mystery.

Legends of the pinelands cling to Brindle Town's vicinity. Charles Remine, who succeeded his father as an undertaker in Wrightstown, remembers the stories well. One anecdote concerns an old colored man, "Nigger Ben," who died several years ago. Ben was said to have been a slave, but the Pineys remembered that he had two stout horns growing out of his temples. The strength of these horns was enough to break down a wooden door. At the old parties, the dancers used to take up a purse and present it to the old darkey, who, they swear, would butt his way through any wooden barricade.

The deserted mill and hotel on the lake at Brindle Town before the town became a part of the expanding Fort Dix reservation.

The schoolhouse-church of Cranberry Hall, unused and windowless for many years has now completely disappeared

XVII

END OF THE WORLD: CRANBERRY HALL

CRANBERRY HALL belies its name. It is a name, which, when you hear it, gives you a picture of an old manor house, blood-red brick and ivy-clad, set far back on a grassy terrace, with a lane of stately maples leading to a Colonial door. As a matter of fact, Cranberry Hall is the remnant of a town, not far back of restored Camp Dix and Wrightstown, a desolate place of ramshackle buildings where a few souls seem to enjoy their own hopelessness. It is really the end of the world.

Only the older maps locate Cranberry Hall, and a few miles above it, Cranberry Park. At the edge of the pine belt, it is in a section which boasts almost any kind of soil that can be found anywhere—sand, loam, clay and even muck. The type of soil that predominates in Cranberry Hall proper, however, is expertly designated as Lakewood sand.

It is obvious that Cranberry Hall obtained its name from an industry that once prospered in its domains. When capital was invested hopefully in a business that pays little these days in this particular area, workers gathered together into a community. We found no authentic record to prove when the town was definitely established.

No mention of Cranberry Hall can be discovered in older records of Hanover Township which enumerate such places as Scrabbletown and Plattsburg, now known as Sykesville. Recent maps fail to take account of it at all.

Between old records and days of modern maps, it had a heyday all its own, just the same.

With bog laborers arriving, buildings were in demand. There were small houses and in their midst the store. In the store lived the man who worked as overseer for the bog owner. This establishment at Cranberry Hall, and even at other bog towns, wasn't the kind we think of today. There was rarely an exchange of money. Moreover, any desire you might have had for luxuries would have gone unheeded. Sugar, tea, coffee, salt pork, flour and potatoes made up the full stock. There may have been a couple of extras now and then, but the occasion was rare. Workers would purchase such articles as were needed and a memorandum would be kept all week. On Saturdays the owner of the "plantation" would give his men an order on the store, accepted in lieu of cash.

If, after the costs of food were deducted, there was any amount left over, the storekeeper on some occasions would make change. This never was considered necessary, however, and it is probable that for months the bog workers never saw any money at all.

Old-timers say there were no worries concerning what was missed. There were no motion picture palaces and home was home. Nobody felt he had to leave town for a good time. Little money was spent and consequently little was wanted. Folk of Cranberry Hall saved their earnings for a Saturday night party, when in the dance hall a fiddler would provide lively music for the variety of country steps. When there was no hall available, someone's house would do as well, providing it had one large room.

Such affairs at Cranberry Hall not only attracted the town's own residents, but also the citizenry of neighboring villages who would wend their way through the woods in wagons and carryalls, combining their enjoyment of an evening's fun with two romantic trips through moonlit woodlands.

The flowing bowl bubbled freely. Liquor, excellent liquor, sold for fifty cents a quart. There were few orgies, it is recalled, and everybody seemed to know when enough was enough.

Sundays were visiting days. "Pineys" and others would gather first at church and later in private homes for long talks and discussion of the news, which, though it did not have to travel far, was a long while in arriving. Few newspapers were seen and only by word of mouth did the more important items receive attention. Monday morning all hands would be back, ready for long hours, every day, rain or shine, until another Saturday noon.

There is a tradition among the Pineys that a certain Saturday afternoon in the calendar is unlucky if one is caught working. To be found laboring in the bogs at such a time is supposed to cause the loss of sight. The Pineys neglected to find out, or else never revealed, just which Saturday is the fatal one, and consequently, they would never work after noon on any Saturday at any time during the year, fearing, as they soberly said, that they might go blind.

So, Cranberry Hall was established. First came the foreman's house and then the new store. Then came the storehouse for the berries. Finally the church and school were erected as one combination building. Life became a grind, certain things to do at certain times. Beyond that? Well, the world was out there somewhere. To go to the city was a longing that might be, with long odds, fulfilled some day. If not, what matter?

One of the leaders of the village was recalled to us as Witten Harker. Everybody knew Uncle Witten. He was tall, gaunt, and smooth-faced, with a kindly disposition, but no especial urge for work. He had a little garden and kept it free of weeds, when the thought occurred to him. Mostly he wandered among his brethren, wearing a long-tailed coat and a dicer, exhorting his fellows to lead more righteous lives.

Uncle Witten came to be much in demand. His dignity meant something to Cranberry Hall. Its townsfolk needed encouragement and cheerful words. He not only preached in the church, as Warner Hargrove recalled hearing him once, but was called on to pray for the sick and recite high-sounding eulogies at funerals. He may have had some credentials as a minister but nobody thought to ask.

It was about 1870 that George B. Cope came to Cranberry Hall, purchasing several hundred acres of land, and established himself as a farmer. He spent a great deal of money in clearing the land, ploughing fields, buying stock and building an imposing home. Cope was an enterprising newcomer who put up the first fences ever seen in the section, planning the planting for his fields. With his several sons and daughters, he sought the comfort of a secluded home.

Cope established a sawmill at Brown's Mills and another at Hanover Furnace, but his best dreams were never realized. The timber supply ran short and the mills were soon abandoned. The type of soil in the neighborhood made the farm unprofitable. Sad at heart and soul-weary, Cope died in the midst of his shattered hopes and his family moved on elsewhere.

If ever you are at Delaware Water Gap and you run

across a hotelman by the name of Cope, ask him about Cranberry Hall. You'll find him a member of the family, no doubt. Other kinsfolk, engaged in the same work, will also be found in Atlantic City.

Eventually the Cope mansion, long deserted, was mysteriously set afire and burned to the ground. Not so long ago the ruin with all the clutter of fields surrounding it, costing thousands of dollars, was sold at public sale for a mere $500.

Today the last of Cope's place will be found on a rise of hill between Cranberry Hall proper and Brown's Mills on a winding uncertain road. The fields where cattle once fed contentedly are going back to the woods. There is only a yawning hole, lined with bricks and bits of mortar, to show where the house itself stood. Not far behind is the tiny track of the donkey railroad of Camp Dix.

It was not an unpleasant afternoon that we chose for visiting Cranberry Hall, but the utter desolation of the place, with something of foreboding, was in the air. It was as if one had reached some uncanny impasse, as if there were no more to be looked for, as if this were the moment for reckoning. There is, or was, at any rate, an eerie finality about everything at Cranberry Hall.

Some of the old houses, shabby, weather-beaten by winter storms and summer sun, hang at the edge of the scraggly "main street" as if they expect something to happen at any moment. The old store is now a house. The church-school is barren and windowless, its old blackboards showing through the apertures. There is no need for either school or church now. The few pupils in town are transported by bus elsewhere for their education.

A loose-jointed angular man sauntered into the road.

Names do not matter in Cranberry Hall. After a try at remembering, he recalled Warner Hargrove, who was with us. They went to school together.

"What have you been doing?" was the question Warner asked.

"Well, nothin' just now," was the reply. "I have been workin' at this and that. But I was laid off yesterday."

"Pretty poor?"

"Poor's a snake," was the answer. "But I guess I'll get along for a month yet, maybe. I've got this far."

Off at the end of the road came another older man, a little stooped, walking with a cane and with one arm in a dirty sling. Warner remembered him, too. He had been in Cranberry Hall in the old days, long before everybody began to die or disappear.

"Haven't been well for a long time," he grumbled, as we came up with him. He sat on a bench, one of innumerable pieces of furniture scattered around the blackish houses on the barren ground. "Had a stroke. Can't use my arm. If I knew my family was going to have so much trouble I wouldn't have married into it." He laughed at his own crazy joke.

Two soldiers, lazily spending their leave from Camp Dix in front of the store of olden days, laughed a little too. From the house came a slovenly girl, broad-featured, a baby in her arms, carpet slippers on her feet.

We sped back to Wrightstown.

XVIII

SWEETWATER

BELOW Indian Mills, between Atsion and Batsto, there's a narrow sliver of road which upon the map mostly follows the line dividing Burlington and Atlantic Counties. If you are over-cautious, wary of scratching whatever vehicle you may use against the brush that walls in the pathway, you will not risk it. But if your mind is bent on adventure and, perhaps, romance, you will follow the twisted, leafy corridor to where, suddenly, you emerge on the shore of Batsto Lake in the town's backyards.

Beyond Atsion you will pass a little white chapel set on a hill with the contrasting unpainted dwellings opposite. From then on you will see many things, deer leaping gracefully through fire-blacked woodlands, less cautious and more inquiring spotted fawns, long-legged white birds in the lowlands above the lake, flaming-red lilies that spring from charred ground and then, at the last, the tree-cloistered and contented town itself. Three times our inquiries led us down that ribbon of road and not once did we meet another human.

Up the trail in the direction of Wescoatville is Pleasant Mills, once Sweetwater, still lapped by the waters of Lake Nescochague as it was in early days when strangers in a new land paused there to thank God for a long-desired freedom. The history of Pleasant Mills goes back to the years before 1685 when the Stuart kings were making war upon the Scottish Kirk with that peculiar nastiness which even in these modern days identifies church controversies. It was in 1685 that George Scott led a group of men and women, who had tired of resisting as Covenanters, to seek the welcome of New Jersey's Quakers.

Baxters, MacGillams, Pecks and Campbells were in an exiled company which in 1707 formed a village near what was the Indian town, Nescochague. Here, as the late C. M. Green, of Hammonton, has pointed out, too enthusiastically perhaps, they found "the harbors of Scotland, the fertility of England and the climate of France, with the forests, the game, the fish, the fruits and freedom of America, beside the curious, clear water which flowed into abundant brooks and runlets."

The first building completed was a rude chapel, constructed of logs. The floor was clay and the roof a thatch of dried grass. Cabins were soon constructed close by, cleared land was quickly planted and cloth, gunpowder and other necessaries of the pioneer, began coming down the Indian trail on pack horses.

It was in the 1750s that a man named Jack Mullin built a sawmill at Nescochague and found business profitable until Revolutionary days. He pulled down and prepared the timber which was used in the first cottages replacing the first early line of rude cabins whose builders already slept in the plot beside the chapel. Today the site of Jack Mullin's Mill is marked by an unkempt rock garden, a pile of Jersey sandstone that may have been part of its foundations. Beside it is a little inscribed marker telling you that Mullin was a patriot and that when the time came he dismantled his mill so that his saws could be forged into broadswords for American cavalrymen.

It was about 1762 that a newcomer, said to be a British

gentleman of fortune, arrived in the tiny community and erected from Mullin's lumber a stately mansion but a stone's throw away, beside the lake. The place was furnished in lavish but dignified Colonial style, a setting for the days of charm, culture and hospitality that were to ensue there. Today, more than 170 years after, the house stands among the relics of the years when it bestowed its name, "Sweetwater," to the town that clustered around it.

According to the best of information obtained by Mr. Green, the builder of "Sweetwater" was named Reid. He had one daughter, a girl of resolute character and rare beauty. It must have been she, Honoria Reid, who served as the heroine, "Kate Aylesford," of the celebrated Peterson novel recounting her adventures among the Refugees. Kate, those who have read the book may remember, was wooed and wed by a doughty soldier, Major Gordon, in 1780. It was in 1782, according to the actual records, that Honoria Reid and an American officer were married.

Sweetwater, the town, prospered. The Indian trail was abandoned for a new stage road connecting with a broader highway at Hammonton Lake, the Hammonton road of today. The old chapel built by the first settlers had become too small for its devoted congregation. In consequence a larger place of worship was constructed by a Presbyterian, Captain Elijah Clark, a veteran of the French and Indian War, who presented it to the folk of Sweetwater. With the coming of the Revolution, Captain Clark was commissioned as an officer, but after two years, he resigned to serve in the Assembly.

As early as 1645 the Reverend John Camanius, a Lutheran minister from Stockholm, arrived as a sort of missionary to the Indians, the Leni Lenapes. Although he was popular among these natives, the work of Mr. Camanius seems to have been wasted and it was not until one hundred years after that tangible progress came.

It was then that David Brainerd arrived. According to records, in four years Brainerd had made converts of all the tribesmen of the locality. John Brainerd, who succeeded David, was pastor at Cold Spring in 1769. In 1774, his diary says, he visited Clark's meeting house at Sweetwater. He must have been impressed by the place for he gives it detailed description, making special mention of the large cedar beams in the church. David Brainerd's work, which surely should be placed in equal importance to that of Father Marquette or John Eliot, took him among the Indians from Kinderhook, N. Y., deep down the Delaware Valley and then to Nescochague Lake.

These first preachers rarely spared themselves. They traveled early and late through woodlands, over mountains, plodding slowly but surely, no distance too great, no task unimportant. At the last, working from his little church at Crossweeksung, now Crosswicks (The Place of Women), Brainerd's health failed and he returned home to New England. There he died in 1747 at the age of twenty-nine. On the site of the first churches, destroyed eventually by forest fires, there is another today, built in 1808. For more than one hundred years it has defied the menace which has quickly obliterated all trace of those colorful religious beginnings.

The rise of Methodism was responsible for this larger building, still used with pious regularity. When a new church was needed because of the growing group of worshipers in Batsto and Sweetwater, the people of the twin villages decided that one structure would best serve their needs. Having formed a board of trustees and obtaining a plot from the Richards, the church was completed in three months. In January, 1809, it was personally dedicated by Francis Asbury, first Methodist Bishop in America.

It is here that our narrative refreshingly swings from the humdrum of historic fact to the romance of legend and folk lore. One of the first pastors of the church was the Rev. Simon Lucas, an austere and opinionated fellow who guarded Sweetwater's religious devotions for many years.

The Rev. Simon had been a Revolutionary soldier and was used to the discipline of the army, at least in the way of receiving and giving orders. With such pioneers as Richards, Gibson Ashcraft, George Peterson, Laurance Peterson and John Morgan at his side, he soon made a name for himself. He believed, among other things, that there was actual danger lurking in the vanities of this world. He said that showy dress, if it must be worn at all, need not be brought into church to distract people from the business of worship for which they had convened.

One day a young woman from another village appeared in church in the glory of gay furbelows and a decorated bonnet that made the girls of Sweetwater wonder who she was. Confident, haughty, bent perhaps on showing these strangers how one could heed fashion's decrees further up the road, she made the mistake of seating herself directly before the pulpit. Brother Lucas rose to announce the opening hymn. As he did, he saw the stranger. His gaze was caught more, however, by a flashing brooch she wore.

"Young woman," said Simon Lucas, "do you know that shiny thing on your dress reminds me of the devil's eye?"

The girl fidgeted and fumed. Finally, flustered and blushing, she left the church. The Rev. Simon, his duty done, bellowed loudly through the first verse of the hymn.

On another occasion, the Atsion Creek was full of a heavy run of herring. Residents of Sweetwater, moreover, depended largely on fish for winter sustenance. As the tide receded, the stream was so full that flapping fish were all along its banks. It was Sunday and no doubt the demure daughter of Jesse Richards, well acquainted with the Rev. Simon's attitude toward many such things, wondered what he would say to those who were fishing on the Lord's Day.

The girl, easily shocked or bent on mischief, addressed her father, saying, "Papa, why don't you stop those men from fishing on Sunday?" Jesse Richards said he wasn't sure he had the right but promised to ask Brother Lucas what he thought.

After service, on the way home, the girl questioned her father concerning what the preacher had said about Sabbath fishing. But the Rev. Simon had proved himself broadly practical as well as strict when occasion demanded.

"Well," he had said to Richards, "the time to catch herring is when the herring are there to catch."

It was from 1826 to 1831 that the Rev. Charles Pitman, poet-preacher of South Jersey for whom Pitman is named, presided as Elder of the West Jersey District. Because of the picturesqueness of the town, giving the church a peaceful and religious aspect apart from the country around it, Pleasant Mills was usually chosen for conferences. Methodist workers rode in for more than fifty miles to these meetings, setting up tents in the clearing around the church when houses of the town could not accommodate the great influx.

The last member of the old West Jersey conference was one Ben Doughty, right-hand man of Pleasant Mills pastors and hospitable host to all who passed that way. He served as trustee, steward and Sunday school superintendent for fifty-two years, dying in 1886.

Methodists, of course, predominated in the neighborhood, but there was a group of Roman Catholics whose number thereabouts was unusual for such a period. Jesse Richards donated a building site, contributed funds and materially aided the erection of the Church of St. Mary of the Assumption. There is no trace of the church today although its burial plot may still be found, a reminder of famous individuals, priests and laymen, who met and ministered there. The church was burned in a forest fire in 1900.

The little graveyard beside the Pleasant Mills Church is really a story all by itself. Beside the pathway leading through the sequestered plot is a small stone inscribed with the name, John Lynch, who at twenty-six, died in the year of the church's building, 1808.

Lynch was a carpenter, a young man of unusual good looks and, according to the story that has been handed down, a devil with the women. Lynch was at work on the roof of the church on a chilly day in December when suddenly, in the act of blowing upon his fingers to warm them, he came tumbling to the ground. He never moved, once his body had struck the ground. Companions who rushed to his side found his neck had been broken. But it was not until long after his death that the rest of the story was revealed.

It seems that Lynch was betrothed to a young woman of the village who had not learned that it is not wise to care for anything very deeply lest, in losing or failing to attain it, life is bereft of all hope. Her affection must have been greater than John's for with the appearance of a new face, the troth they had plighted was forgotten. The girl, who-ever she was, made overtures that got her nowhere. Finally, beside herself and distracted, she exclaimed "I do hope John Lynch dies before that church is finished." Later comparisons showed that it was at exactly this moment that John, the carpenter, came tumbling to his death.

John Lynch was buried beside the church whose com-pletion he never saw. Somewhere near, unidentified among the host of names on the quaint stones, is the grave of the girl, who, clad in the mourning that bespoke the remorse she felt for the sudden and unexpected gratifying of her thoughtless wish, died of a broken heart. With these two lie the founders of old Sweetwater as well as veterans of Valley Forge, of Trenton, Princeton, and 1812.

Nearest the church and enclosed by a small picket fence is the plot of the Richards family, chiefly distinguished by an odd-shaped vault, the grave of Jesse Richards. Near-by are the names of other kin, whose markers bear dates from 1788 to 1811. Just outside is a carefully shaped Jersey sandstone inscribed with the name of Captain John Keeny, an officer of the French and Indian War, who died in 1760.

Captain Keeny, a Scotchman, died while on a visit to his old comrade in arms, Elijah Clark, who arranged an impressive funeral. The oldest grave in the yard is a few feet to the east, and is that of Benjamin Peck, who died in 1732, leaving behind him this quaint admonishment:

> "Trust not to glit'ring
>   Prospecks, ohe wife,
>   Nor hope for perfect
>   Hapiness below the skye."

You will also take note of the grave of Nicholas Sooy, mine host of the Washington Tavern, once a recruiting station for Washington's forces. A plain headstone over the resting place of Abbigail Miner informs you that she was the wife of John Faning of Connecticut, and the mother of three sons who with their father perished in the service of the American Navy. Beside the stones of Borick Mick, who died in 1794, Simon Lucas himself, Chockie Leek, the numerous Wescoats of Wescoatville, and Gemima Thompson, is that of a Mrs. Tyler, which reads:

"In memory of Parnell Tyler,
late wife and widow
in their turn to Paul Sears
and William Coffan, Dec'd."

The Doughtys, Lipsetts, Sooys, Etheridges, Fanings and Birdsalls are names which on the stones, of cobbles, marble, iron from the Batsto furnace and even a chunk of hand-graven washstand, take Pleasant Mills back to its earliest days of Sweetwater.

In 1821 a cotton mill containing three thousand spindles was built by William Lippincott, a brother-in-law of Jesse Richards. The plant was named "The Pleasant Mills of Sweetwater" from which title the town's modern name has since been derived. The place was in operation thirty-five years, giving work to many and considerable profit to its owner.

The cotton mill was not rebuilt after a fire in 1856. From its ruin, however, a paper mill sprang up in 1861, placed in motion by Irving and MacNeil and later a third man, John Farrell. In three years the first two sold out to the third,

moving on to Weymouth. Farrell and his son William continued the business as the Nescochague Manufacturing
Company until the autumn of 1878 when the place again
was leveled by a fire. The present structure, now in disuse,
was put up in 1880 by the Pleasant Mills Paper Company,
a concern organized by the younger Farrell and Herman
Hoopes. Since that time there has been a series of names
as owners and operators.

Farrell died in 1893 and his property, bequeathed to his
wife, was sought by his relatives. The business went to pot,
operating under a receiver, Howard Cooper, until the
courts gave a decision in favor of Mrs. Farrell, who afterward married L. M. Cresse, of Ocean City. Cresse, who
acted as president of the concern, died in 1914 and a year
later his widow closed the business after thirty-four years
of turning wheels by the lake spillway. A. J. McKeone
purchased the mill in 1917, taking up residence in the mansion, "Sweetwater."

The mill is deserted today. "No Admittance" and "Ap-
ply to Owner" signs are nailed to its doors and windows.
Behind in the long grass beside the mill hole there are soggy
masses of cardboard and paper. Inside the office is scattered a litter of official-looking papers, stationery and let-
terheads, most of them bearing the name of one of the
periodic operators, the Norristown Magnesia and Asbestos
Company. An old safe, its doors wide, sags drunkenly to
the floor.

From the lake shore of Sweetwater have come illustrious
men, among them Joseph Fralinger, of Atlantic City, once
a glassblower, later one of the earliest baseball promoters
and organizer of the "August Flower Nine." Gen. St.
Clair Mulholland, who used to listen to "Uncle Joe" John-

son at Pleasant Mills when he told of how he fired the first shot at Bunker Hill, was another who was born in the quaint, quiet old town.

In 1914, Kate Aylesford Chapter, D.A.R., dignified the community and commemorated soldiers and sailors in its cemetery with a bronze tablet placed inside the church. No memorial will ever adequately serve, however, as a tribute to those days of old and the people who lived in them. One is reluctant to leave this old town, its backwoods bog roads, its tiny church and its park for which admission now is charged. The watchful eyes of Warden George Adams peer out across the woods from the Batsto tower, in search of smoke. While he watches we can close with one more story, a favorite of the Atlantic County historian:

Among the colorful characters whose mortal remains lie without specific testimonial in the Pleasant Mills yard was Jack Van Dyke, seaman and master of the *Gypsy Jane*, as well as an expert in profanity. In the old days of the West Indian trade he was Lucky Jack Van Dyke, for his cargoes were rich, his port calls regular. Then a British frigate came along and Jack and his crew were made prisoners.

Cap'n Jack then let loose a streak of vitriolic syllables that consigned King George, his Navy, his sailors and such wandering marauders as the British captain, to places where temperatures are never so cool as those at Sweetwater. The English master, courteous and dignified, objected and bade Lucky Van Dyke to speak of eminent personages and institutions in more respectful terms.

For reply Cap'n Jack opened up: "Damn the King and double-damn him and damn the man who wouldn't damn him!" he shouted.

The Britisher found himself compelled to laugh. Soon

he and Van Dyke became staunch friends. When Jack was released he was wished better luck next time. Van Dyke merely answered: "Have no fear of that, sir. Be sure I'll get my back pay and King George will be the paymaster." And Lucky Van Dyke captured a British merchantman soon after, the story goes.

As secrets of Sweetwater's charm become known, old and revered relics must become a bit tarnished. Already one of the dwellings that served a paper-maker of long ago is a rude bathhouse. Already there is a new commercial spirit, far different from the bustle of the mill and the patriotic devotion which turned its saws into swords.

The paper mill at Pleasant Mills was started in the 1860's, when mass production of paper was still in the future. With linen and cotton fiber in short supply, the owners tried out straw, bark, hemp, cattail stalks, ground wood, and salt grass.

XIX

OLD HALF WAY

THIS is the story of Old Half Way and Union Clay Works, as you can find them today back in the pines from Wood-mansie station on the Jersey Central.

When the first search for these evasive villages was made, the cars were kept to the rutted trails leading out of Woodmansie, and while evidences of houses were found here and there among the fields of Indian grass, it was not until much later that the full certainty of location came to the searchers.

Both towns have their tattered history linked to still an-other industry of the pines that has gone to pot, that of clay mining. The operations must have been extensive, for to-day the excavations have left behind them tall mounds of gravel, weathered and scarred so that they have the appear-ance of a volcano and its craters. In the soft earth, mottled by vari-colored stones and pebbles, there are the tracks of hundreds of deer—for it is here, out of season, that they come to drink.

The clay pits are reached best straight through from Woodmansie, up the ties of the old narrow-gauge railroad. The rails have been removed and the ties are rotting to pieces. It's a rough road to take in an automobile, but it's the only way to be sure of getting through. The pines have sprung up on either side, almost obscuring the passageway at that. It was a trip of a million bumps, but it was worth while.

The pits themselves are filled with water, a greenish-blue liquid taking its color from the clay deposits. Along the railway line and on top of the gravel mountains, contrasting the surrounding landscape, are bits of rubbish that recall forgotten industry, torn gloves, chunks of coal, rusted pipes and old tobacco cans. The buildings out at Woodmansie, one or two now serving as clubs for deer hunters, are the only formidable relics of this mammoth undertaking that failed.

The pits at Old Half Way show more remains of an actual town. Willis Buzby, of Chatsworth, said that the town itself had been dug up by the clay people and he was right. But at the edge of the diggings, marked as before by the feet of deer down to the waterside, there are domestic trees, a couple of wells, the bricks of one or two houses and a patch of what was once furrowed ground. The place itself is far from anywhere.

But the blight that extends its fingers through the scrub growth of the pinelands has not choked off the activity of wild folk. In fact, Old Half Way seemed to be a kind of bird sanctuary. We saw robins by the score, bluebirds, and a red-winged blackbird. In two of the maples, strangers in the evergreens, there were squirrels' nests. One thought of the loneliness, however, the certainty that life and death could pass here equally unknown.

The town of Union Clay Works must have been some distance from either of the clay operations. Buzby told us that as he drew a rough map of the vicinity, showing the village itself stretching on both sides of the road, and that elusive cemetery some distance through the trees.

The clearing itself is unmistakable. We found the ruins of one house and two of the wells when we stopped to search among those domesticated trees. This time we extended our explorations through the woods at the other side of the trail. We came upon any number of broken sections of terra cotta pipe, one pile draped around what may have been a kiln. This must have been a clearing long ago, for trees have sprung up among the bricks and bits of pipe to varying heights of twenty-five and thirty feet.

This is country in which it is easy to lose oneself. Once we traveled in a complete circle seeking the forsaken graveyard. Only the shout of a companion who had remained on the road brought us back. Then, staging one last invasion, systematically trying out Buzby's map, we tried again. We had walked perhaps a mile through the undergrowth and trees, when four does leaped high across the clearing. Pressing on, one of us suggested going back to the cars when we caught sight of a tombstone.

There are five graves altogether. Two are marked by chunks of Jersey stone. Three have home-made headstones, but they have chipped apart because of their clay-baked base. This condition brought about the invention of the jigsaw tombstone game, in which we tried to put the scattered pieces together to make something of the inscriptions. But it was little use. One of the deceased was named Atkerson—we made that out—and another had a melancholy injunction: "Put away your dresses—you won't need them any more."

Old Half Way and Union Clay Works—they're quite as dead as these stones and those who lie forgotten beneath them.

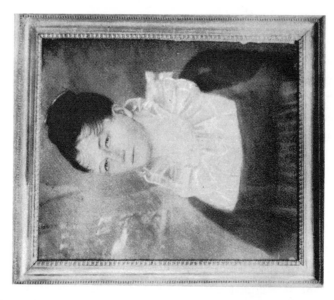

Judge Joshua Brick, pioneer industrialist of Port Elizabeth, and his wife, Ellen Lee Brick. Pastels in the collection of the late Senator Robert R. McAllister of Bridgeton.

XX

PORT ELIZABETH: A WOMAN'S TOWN

A BRONZE tablet attached to an ancient buttonwood in the Friends' Cemetery in Haddonfield is inscribed as a memorial to Elizabeth Haddon, founder of the town. Her character has been celebrated not only by historians, but by the poet Longfellow, in his *Tales of a Wayside Inn*.

Beneath a forgotten little stone in another Quaker burying ground, not so far away as distances go these days, are the mortal remains of another woman who built a town, a woman who for too many passersby, hides her identity behind the inscribed initials, "E. B."

The legend goes that these were two Elizabeths who were great friends and that they journeyed to each other's town in alternate years for Quarterly Meeting. Elizabeth Haddon, later Estaugh, was more likely the inspiration of Elizabeth Bodly, founder of Port Elizabeth. For when Mrs. Bodly was first married, at the age of twenty, in 1757, Elizabeth Estaugh was sixty-four.

Port Elizabeth has become, to those who hustle through the village on their way to shore resorts, just another of tiny towns along the road. And yet, though its dreams have long ago been broken, its memories are still vividly alive.

You would not think, for instance, that in days of long ago, Port Elizabeth was the most important center in its area, that it claimed a distinction, in industry, in world commerce and in social activity beyond the dreams of glassmaking Millville, its present neighbor. You would not think that this tiny landing on the Maurice River was a port of delivery, that vessels plied directly from here to the West Indies, that here there were manufacturing enterprises of which there is now little trace. But such are the facts.

In our journey through the town and the farmlands surrounding it, we came upon a blue-eyed, brown-skinned tiller of the soil who told us, among other things, that he and his friends are going to try and put a monument on Elizabeth Bodly's grave some day. By the fulfillment of such an ambition he can render a service to an old town which in the press of modern hurly-burly is fast losing its individuality.

This farmer told us, too, that Elizabeth Bodly was very probably Swedish royalty and that she must have sought to lose herself in the new land, taking a new name and hiding away in a corner of Cumberland County. In this, however, he was probably wrong. Elizabeth Bodly was the daughter of John Ray and was born in Pilesgrove Township, Salem County, in 1737, twenty-five years after Elizabeth Haddon had built her first Haddonfield manor house.

Elizabeth Ray married Cornelius Clark, a native of Burlington, and soon after, went to live on a large tract of land they purchased on the Manumuskin Creek. Calling a little log house their home, four children were born—Joel, John, Susan and Elizabeth. Their father died young and their mother, left to fend for herself, her farm and her children, proved equal to the task, harvesting from the best meadowland in the vicinity.

John Bodly, admiring the assurance and the resolute personality as well as the charm of such a pioneer, became Elizabeth's second husband. There were two more children,

Sarah and Mary, and then Mrs. Bodly found herself a widow once more.

For Elizabeth, life was no bed of roses and death a too-frequent visitor. Two husbands had died. Joel, the eldest son of Cornelius Clark, married Ann Dallas and died shortly after. John, the second son, died of camp fever while in his country's service during the Whisky Rebellion. Susan, the eldest daughter, married Jonathan Dallas, and died a few months later. Mary married Maurice Beesley, who died before his son, Theophilus, later a Salem physician, reached his 'teens.

In the face of these troubles, Elizabeth struggled on. She was a large woman, with coal-black eyes and a smooth complexion, called handsome even in her last years. She was the friend of all and it is probable that in her day there was no one who did not know that friendship or hospitality. When winter came, in those early days, the intense cold found many unprepared in this strange land. Elizabeth cared for them, her portico continually crowded by those in need.

Picture her, in passing, in her Quaker bonnet and shawl, her grandchildren at her knee, listening as some wayfarer told a tinseled tale of goblins and witches. When such transients had departed she would tell her progeny that there was nothing to such stories, that she had listened, spellbound, merely to be polite. Her life, eventful, useful, and a triumph over adversity and sorrow, came to an end November 25, 1815, at the age of seventy-eight. And so her name clings to a village which in every way was her own.

From the cluster of log houses Elizabeth Bodly found upon the Manumuskin, Port Elizabeth grew to be a thriving community. She had employed surveyors to plot the village, bounded on the north by Broadway, on the east by Second Street, on the south by Lombard or Quaker Street, and on the west by Front Street. In 1789 an Act of Congress established a district for the collection of duties on imports at Bridgeton, making Port Elizabeth and Salem, seemingly of equal size at that time, the ports of delivery.

James and Thomas Lee, Joshua Brick, Isaac Townsend and Stephen Willis were among the first young business men who saw Port Elizabeth's advantages, purchasing lots, setting up dwellings and building storehouses for lumber shipping and other commercial pursuits. The growth was steady and promising. Vessels arrived from and sailed away to the West Indies until the greater facilities of New York and Philadelphia eliminated them as trade centers. Port Elizabeth in the early 1800s was one of the two leading towns in the County, Bridgeton claiming equal prominence.

When we visited Port Elizabeth, it was necessary to make a slow, dusty detour through an iron bridge beside a high mound of earth upon which now rests a new span, part of the State highway system. Port Elizabeth did not like this latest evidence of progress, and no wonder. Although the new bridge undoubtedly speeds traffic and aids the modern credo of incessant rush, it has destroyed forever the town's ancient aspect, just as does a high wall built around a garden. As the iron span of other years obliterated a covered crossing, the new concrete structure blots out another milestone.

Port Elizabeth set up its own Post Office in 1802 in a nest of comfortable homes and hotels for commercial travelers. What was called the Old Hotel stood between David

Lore's store and the home of Francis Lee, and was operated as early as 1788 by Benoni Dare. Mary Beesley, daughter of Elizabeth Bodly, opened another at Broadway and Front Street. A fire in May, 1883, destroyed what there was of this much-altered inn and no hotel has been operated in Port Elizabeth since that time.

Christian Stanger opened a hotel at the Eagle Glass-Works in 1807. The ground for this glass-making establishment, traceable by deeds from Abram Jones in 1782, was sold by Nathan Hand in 1805 to James Lee, 177 acres for two thousand dollars. But the factories had been built by Lee previous to 1799 and continued to operate under different managements until 1884.

Of the glass pits, the kilns and the remnants of products, there is no sign on the site. Such, too, is the end of the old Union Glass Works, once on the north bank of the Manumuskin. After a court wrangle and the appointment of Joshua Brick, Isaac Townsend and Stephen Willis to distribute the property, there was a fire, and several years after, "on a clear still day" as the records say, the ruins tumbled in a heap. Although there had been a hotel at the Eagle plant, called Glasstown, there was none at Union. There were hostelries, however, at Bricksboro, to the south, and near the Spring Garden Ferry House.

Port Elizabeth was celebrated at one time as one of the most important educational centers of the country. As early as June 30, 1798, Mrs. Bodly had deeded to the trustees of the Federal School a portion of the present school lot, now occupied by a substantial building erected in 1854. In addition to the several private schools that were operated from time to time, there was established the Port Elizabeth Academy, founded by a company which included Thomas Lee, Joshua Brick, Dr. Benjamin Fisler and others. This school, called the most elaborate in South Jersey in its heyday, was in operation prior to 1810.

Students came from far. Only the best teachers were employed on the Academy's staff. Sciences, fine arts and languages were taught, but as other institutions of learning were created and gained reputation, the Port Elizabeth Academy went into decline. Years after abandonment, its building was purchased and dedicated, in 1846, as a Roman Catholic Church, by Father Gartland, a Philadelphia priest, who later became Bishop of Charleston, S. C. As a church it did not continue long, and in 1878 the old building, worn and weather-beaten, was removed to Dennis Creek in Cape May County.

From its earliest beginnings Port Elizabeth correlated its growth with the development of religious life. During its existence it has had Methodist, Friends, Presbyterian, Baptist and African Methodist congregations.

The Methodist Church had a colorful start. In 1773 Benjamin Abbott, a resident of Pittsgrove Township, Salem County, joined the Methodists and became an evangelist. Among those early pioneers Abbott must have been an unusual fellow. Up to the age of forty, he led a riotous life and was a leader in everything improper and contrary to church teaching. He attended a Quarterly Meeting at Port Elizabeth, and his life at once was changed. He threw down the scythe, turned over a new leaf and began to preach with fire and fury. The organization of the church in Port Elizabeth dates from his time.

When William Donnelly, a local Methodist circuit-rider residing in Port Elizabeth, died, a burial plot was provided for him by Elizabeth Bodly. A church had been urged but had not been built as yet. However, Donnelly's work bore fruit in the definite building of a place of worship, a frame structure, in 1786. A brick edifice replaced it in 1827, and this building, surrounded by the graves of a town's pioneers, still stands. A tower which surmounts it was not part of the original plan, but was erected to hold a bell hung in memory of twelve Port Elizabeth men who served in the World War.

The graveyard has some of the infinite calm and quietude of old St. Peter's, Old Swedes, or Christ Church, in Philadelphia. Among the stones that have withstood time and storm on the high bank of the Manumuskin, one is apart from the workaday world. Pioneers of yesteryear and famous men lie here.

Upon one stone is written the name of Benjamin F. Mitchell, a member of company H, 4th N. J. Volunteers, who was wounded at Gaines Mill and died in prison June 27, 1862. John J. Mitchell, of Company K, is beside him. Next is Captain Richard D. Mitchell, of the Second N. J. Cavalry, who perished from yellow fever in New Orleans in 1878. Another Civil War veteran, William M. Mitchell, who died in Hamilton, Ontario, Canada, completes the group.

There are the graves near by of Joshua Brick, Esq., who died in 1791; his son, Joshua, who died in 1860, and Ellen Brick, who dying in 1820, lay claim to this quaint inscription: "Life, how short; eternity, how long!" Of Reuben Willets, who at fifty-seven, died in 1858, the marker says to all who pass: "He was a good man." "Precious in the sight of the Lord are the deaths of his saints," testifies the stone of Hannah E. Willets, who died at eighty-seven in 1893.

Among the Willetses is Colonel J. Howard, who in serving with the Twelfth N. J. Infantry, fought at Antietam and was wounded at Chancellorsville, Va. Despite his high rank, he was but twenty-nine at the time of the battle, having graduated with honors at West Point. He died in 1927.

Among the older and more unusual stones are those of Hopey Simmons; William Jones, who died in 1798; Azariah Foster, who died in 1799; Irving Lee, 1801-1899; Elizabeth Lore, who at sixty died in 1761; and Hezekiah, "his consort," who at seventy-three died in 1770. A stone flush against the church building marks the resting place of Rev. Richard Swain, who at forty-five died in 1808. Beside him is "his consort," Charity. Of the preacher is written: "He traveled preaching the gospel about fifteen years and lingered out five years more in great weakness of body, but left this world in a triumph of faith."

Among its early business enterprises Port Elizabeth numbered two tanneries, one begun in 1799 by John Coombs and Randall Marshall, and another, known as the Old Silvers Tannery, which was in business in 1818. Isaac Townsend kept a store. David Lore was proprietor of another. Francis Lee operated still another shop at Second Street and Broadway. Perhaps the greatest industrial endeavor was undertaken in 1837 when Isaac Townsend, Thomas Lee, Joshua Brick and others formed the Port Elizabeth Manufacturing Company which purposed "to manufacture cotton, wool, silk and iron and also to dye, print and bleach cotton fabrics." Though a charter was granted no business was ever transacted.

Two explanations are currently given for the passing of Port Elizabeth, and the relegation to the scrap heap of its industries, activities and prosperity. One is that the railroad was to blame. The Pennsylvania, lining out its tracks, cut through to Millville and avoided Port Elizabeth, thus booming Millville as the center Port Elizabeth expected to be. Another version is that the glass pioneers, seeking tracts of land on which to place larger and more modern plants, were refused property at reasonable price in Port Elizabeth, and so went further up the road, to Millville.

Of the many unusual legends and stories one always finds in forgotten towns it is necessary to select only a few for recounting here. One concerns the "Negro Exodus" of 1824 when Captain Samuel Craig, who ran a packet from Port Elizabeth to Philadelphia, gathered up two shiploads of Negroes and bringing them to the Port, transferred them to the schooner *Olive Branch* on which they were shipped to "Hayti." Finding stories of delicacies that grew there without cultivation, and promises of a new black man's kingdom were idle gossip, many died in disappointment. Ned Wright and John Cornish, two of the adventurers, returned later, however, to Port Elizabeth.

There is an anecdote connected with the "exodus" which links it to the legend of a haunted hotel, the hostelry which once stood across the street from the impressive old residence of the late Colonel Willets. Here, today, there is a gasoline filling station which all but hides the spring house which was once the hotel's. It seems that in 1817-1818 the haunted hotel caused some concern. Every night at dusk there was a terrible commotion. Windows began to rattle and finally, the whole neighborhood turned out to witness the strange manifestations and obtain, if possible, some explanation.

At last a colored girl, a servant in the place, was caught, running soundlessly through the rooms, making queer noises, shaking windows and then appearing before the company with an expression of guileless alarm on her face.

In the "exodus" there was a colored girl working for John Ogden at the hotel who sought to sail with the others to Haiti. On being refused permission, she dressed in man's attire and hid aboard the schooner. We have wondered, in passing, if this girl was not the same as she who had terrified the hotel's guests, four years before, and who, on detection, claimed she had been bribed by an old witch.

An article in the *Christian Advocate and Journal*, written by Rev. Mr. Purdue, of Millville, in 1843, concerns one Mary Coombs, whose sister was a devoted member of the Methodist Church at Port Elizabeth. Mary, born in 1794, when about ten was strangely impressed by her mother's reading of the scriptures. Three years later, while at a Methodist Quarterly in Tuckahoe, she experienced what was called "a clear sense of God's pardoning mercy." The change was so great that she told her companions that with the realization of it she had "neither troubles nor trials."

On the twentieth of November, 1808, she fell into a strange spell, in which she remained for seven days and nights. The muscular fibre of her body became rigid, the extremities became numb and cold and consciousness left her except for a brief time, each night at six o'clock. Then, after an uncanny paroxysm of trembling, Mary would speak, beginning usually with the words, "Blessed Jesus." For from thirty to forty-five minutes, the girl exhorted those about her with words that were much beyond her age and education, and a voice that seemed like that of some other person.

It was only natural that as the strange phenomenon was told abroad great excitement should result. Crowds assembled and were chastened by the remarkable voice, the fineness of diction, and the whole inexplicable occurrence. Mary, swallowing but a few spoonfuls of thin gruel, forced between her teeth, over the entire period, regularly regained consciousness each evening, and after the "preaching," slipped back into what resembled a deep sleep.

On the second of these occasions Mary told her hearers that she would speak, to all who would hear, each dusk and that a week from the beginning of her exorcising she would conclude her "work" and return home. The crowd on this final occasion was consequently large. The house was filled with all who had been told of the strange happenings. A physician had been summoned from Bridgeton but he had announced an inability to do anything, stating that he "did not understand the case."

At the conclusion of her talk on the seventh evening, exactly a week from the beginning, November 27, 1808, she seemed to arouse from a calm slumber, and before 500 bewildered persons, left her bed and went about preparations for returning home. The pastor, who afterward chronicled the strange story, said that he had personally interviewed Mary, who had married, he said, and become a Mrs. Surran. Although she was reserved on the subject, she admitted "the words were all put into my mouth and I had to speak them." While speaking, she said she heard the harmony of pleasant sounds as if produced by sweet voices and heavenly choirs. The circumstances precluded collusion.

At old Port Elizabeth, Mrs. Willets, the Colonel's widow, lived in the charming old house next to the closed physician's office at the corner. Inside we found her, glumly considering the new bridge "wall," but smiling and gracious among the recollections of an old town. With her was her daughter, Mrs. Thomas B. Lee, wife of the Cooper Hospital physician, one of the Port's well-known Lees.

Mrs. Lee recalled days when life was a series of adventures in the ruins of the glass works and fields where old Indian camps had left many relics to be found. In the old house, with its grandfather's clock and many other priceless mementoes of the past, Mrs. Lee told of the old Swedish cemetery, where from its cedar-lined banks, a skeleton slips into the waters of the Maurice River now and then.

Port Elizabeth, you see, goes on with its same names handed down since those first years of its picturesque founder. The Lees, the Bricks, the Willetses, Olivers, Lores, Vanamans, and Strattans will go on, long after Port Elizabeth becomes an old story and the wharf at Bricksboro goes the way of the hotels, schools and ferryhouse. In 1885 these descendants of the pioneers went back and held an impressive centennial celebration.

Meanwhile those who find importance in the past as well as the future will gain some solace, possibly, in the lines of C. B. Ogden's poem of the Centennial:

> "Secure in their hands the Old Port shall remain,
> They will guard her best interests and cherish her
> name."

XXI

FORGOTTEN LITTLE PINE MILL

A LITTLE to the north of Brown's Mills, you may find, some day, a long, low building falling into decay, with a dwelling attached at one end.

Here, on a winding, one-car width, wagon-track road is the site of Little Pine Mill—a tiny town which was once the center of industrial activity and nocturnal entertainment.

Older residents of Burlington County who were inclined to enjoy social life in the old days, making the 1860 and 1870 brands of whoopee, remember the big times, the parties and the dances of Little Pine Mill. This was a town where a man could drown his sorrow in the flowing bowl, or key his spirits to lilting tunes from a square-dance fiddler.

It is hard to realize that this low building was the bowling alley, that the dwelling at the end was the barroom and that the needle-carpeted clearing under the trees was the site of the dance hall. It is difficult to believe that here was once a village, a hotel and the requisites that go to make a health resort.

In the old days, a lake had been made by the damming of a stream running through the place, known as Little Pine Run. The pines, taller, finer trees in yesteryear, surrounded the town for miles. At the foot of the lake was erected a sawmill, operated entirely by water power and cutting trees into boards with the old-fashioned up-and-down saw.

Planking at that time was sold and delivered as low as $12 a thousand feet.

One William Vaughan was the sawyer in charge. Everybody knew William as Uncle Billy Van. Billy lived to be a very old man and is remembered for his stories of the things he had seen and heard in Little Pine Mill.

The owner of the property in the mill days was John Coombs. From the profits of the mill—profits, mind you, at $12 a thousand—Coombs erected a boarding-house, a bar, and a large dance pavilion. In conjunction with these he also had built a bowling alley and a refreshment store.

At the bar the very best applejack—Jersey lightning—was sold at five cents a drink, and a drink wasn't a thimble. You could play Ten Pins for ten cents a game. And with bowling, dancing, music and excellent, reasonably priced liquor as attractions, Little Pine Mill became known as a health center.

On Saturday nights, and frequently through the week, the gleam of the dance-hall lanterns flashed into the night. Echoes of the music of fiddle and harp were heard through the woods with the cries of, "Take your partners!" "All hands around!" and "Swing corners!"

A regular attendant at these extremely social functions was Daniel Dennis, and Sally, his wife, a pair of Pineys. It was whispered that Dan had Indian blood in his veins, but nobody ever dreamed of asking him such a personal question. Dan was a dancer, and served for a long time as regular fiddler. He would play at dance-parties in homes near the village, but on many occasions he was in special demand at the Pine Mill hall.

There, he and his wife, Sal, would give exhibitions of dancing. Dan would play the violin and jig at the same time, holding in his teeth a corncob pipe on which he puffed furiously. Sal would join in unrestrainedly, puffing her pipe and flipping her calico skirt to the plaudits of the watchers. Mostly Dan and Sal did their cavorting in bare feet. A collection would be taken up after the finale.

Another family usually associated with the old days at Little Pine Mill was that of Stumpy Joe. Stumpy Joe was the only name by which he was ever known. His family consisted of Stumpy, his wife, Alice, and a whole tribe of little Stumpies, Stumpy Bill, Stumpy Sam, Stumpy Joe, Jr., and Stumpy Sal, all gaining the nickname through their unusually diminutive stature. None wore shoes until severe weather set in.

Stumpy Joe never saw a circus in his life but he was far ahead of the best circus entertainers. Any time you wanted him to or would give him an audience, he would eat a catfish raw! At other times the crowd would contribute to buy Joe a pint of lightning which he would drink at one "drag." Two pints would put him in such spirits that he would offer to kick the bark off a pine tree with his bare feet.

When Stumpy Joe's wife died, he married a younger woman known as Caddie Dink. A new family came into existence, including Alice Dink, Becky Dink, Isa Dink, Elmer Dink, and Billy Dink. After a time Caddie tired of Joe and fell in love with her stepson, Joe-Boy, as they called him. Stumpy Joe didn't like that very much, and one morning they found him where he had hanged himself on a convenient pine.

Old-timers recall that it was at about this time Snapper Bill Dennis, a son of Dan and Sal, the dancers, came into the picture. From then on domestic relations were not so pleasant between Joe-Boy and Caddie. The fact that Caddie had married Joe-Boy and that Snapper Bill already had two wives made no difference. Leander Joyce, village squire of Little Pine Mill, married them without remembering much history.

They told us about the wedding. Snapper Bill wore a new straw hat, a gingham shirt and overalls. Caddie wore her sunbonnet and a calico dress. Neither wore shoes or stockings. After the ceremony they went down the winding trail arm-in-arm, followed by little Dinks and Stumpies.

Their wedded bliss was short-lived. At Mount Holly fair time, Caddie wanted to take all her children. Perhaps this was too expensive for Snapper Bill. At any rate an argument and a separation ensued. Joe-Boy and Stumpy Sal were still living, they told us, Joe an inmate of the County hospital.

Uncle Billy Van used to tell how lumber made at Little Pine Mill was nearly all sold at Bristol, Pa. It was carted out of the woods to Burlington and then taken across the Delaware. There was once a winter so cold, it is remembered, that the ice was thick enough to bear horses and carts, wearing ruts in the frozen surface a foot deep.

Like the story of the watermelon that lasted a family two months in Ong's Hat, Uncle Billy told another that certainly runs the anecdote a close second.

Billy said that once it was so cold they thought they ought to find out how thick the ice was. They cut a hole, he soberly declared, and found that it was sixty-five feet down to the water.

Uncle Billy used to follow that one up with the story of the sleighing party that fell down an airhole in the ice. Cries of gaiety and pleasure were cut short as the vehicle dived from view. A moment later, Uncle Billy swore, the sleigh came up another airhole and its party went on enjoying the trip, a little wet for the experience. Those two stories, retold perhaps more than any others in the section, are always identified with Little Pine Mill.

The old hotel burned down several years ago. The dance hall, haunted with memories, fell into decay and its ruins were quickly covered by the falling pine needles. The lake bottom, after the dam broke and went unrepaired, was used as a cranberry bog but now is a tangled mass. The barroom is just a dwelling. The bowling alley, unpainted and falling apart, is a storehouse for lumber. Little Pine Mill is forgotten.

The dance hall at Little Pine Mill was the scene of merry revels a century ago.

The grave of Joe Mulliner, bandit of the Tuckerton Road, tried, convicted, and hanged in Burlington in 1781.

XXII

JOE MULLINER: THE MAN THEY HANGED

Down on the Mullica River, near the forgotten towns that once were Nescochague and Sweetwater, there is a sturdy cluster of gnarled poplars, standing gaunt against the sky. Here, when the wind is up and the night is pitch-black, strange spirits are abroad. Shouts ride the gale and from a low limb of one of the trees, a body swings to and fro.

In the scrub cedar that borders the river, weird shadows move. Lights flicker and gutter out. The eerie wraith falls, or rather seems to float to the ground. Then it searches for something and, disappointed, strides off down the road to a lonely grave.

The grave is that of Joe Mulliner, South Jersey's Robin Hood, "bad man" and practical joker, who was tracked down and hanged for his many misdeeds.

The Mulliner ghost story, one of the oldest of the pine-lands, is still told at firesides, in the faded villages it concerned. It is years now since the last traveler, racing a lathered mount to Pleasant Mills, told how he had plainly seen Joe Mulliner's phantom, earnestly searching in the dark for the gold he buried long ago. Perhaps Joe found it. Searching parties, organized time and again, never have.

Joe Mulliner was an outlaw of the old Tuckerton stage road and of the pine towns, Quaker Bridge, Washington, Green Bank and Mount, as well as any village with a hotel and a cluster of homes. A rawboned fellow, given to much hearty laughter, he was known to be descended from a good

167

family. Two of his brothers served with honor in the Colonial Army, but Joseph seems to have preferred a life with a different sort of sustained adventure.

There is no proof that he ever killed anyone, or even inflicted bodily injury. He and his gang of outlaws, or "Refugees," as they were called between 1780 and 1782, contented themselves with swooping raids for plunder and the good times that accompanied them. When it came to actually hanging him it was for robbery and traffic with the enemy.

Joe Mulliner's band was only one of a number that plied a nefarious trade through the pine villages. The name "Refugees" was applied because the wanderers professed allegiance to the King, while in reality there was little loyalty to anyone except, perhaps, to themselves.

Mulliner's gang numbered forty and had its headquarters in the Hemlock Swamp not far from Sweetwater. Daring rogues capable of anything gathered here in the night, sometimes masked and at others more daring. On the stroke of midnight they would begin their crusades of deviltry. Seizures of noted persons, demands for ransom and payments of high tribute filled their record books.

In one of Charles J. Peterson's novels there is an account of one of Mulliner's adventures insofar as it concerned Kate Aylesford, heiress of Sweetwater, heroine of the book. Her escape from the outlaws, despite baying bloodhounds set at her heels and her subsequent timely rescue by friends, provide a thrilling chapter to the romance that is believed to have been unexaggerated.

Joe was a handsome man and had been well educated. He liked company and reveled in popularity. His particular weakness was for tavern parties, barn dances, and other such frolics. Usually he would strut into an inn during the midst of festivities, a hand resting easily on a long-muzzled pistol, secure in the knowledge that one of his men would warn him of approaching minions of law and order.

There are any number of stories that link Joe Mulliner to the old forgotten towns. Once there was a widow named Bates who, it is said, owned a small farm near a fork in the road to Washington. Mrs. Bates was a large woman of masculine appearance and an ardent patriot. She had eight sons, four of whom were in General Washington's army. The remaining four, too young to serve, helped their mother in cultivating the fields of the farm and earning a comfortable livelihood.

Returning from meeting one Sunday afternoon with her boys, the widow found her farm in the possession of Mulliner's gang. Joe himself was not with the company, and so the house had been ransacked of rare furniture and silver plate. The marauders had freely helped themselves to the larder as well as to pigs and poultry from the surrounding fields.

The widow might have let things pass, but when she spied her silverware among the goods the gang had packed for carrying away, she let loose a fury of words which allowed no interruption. The leader loudly bade her to hold her tongue under threat of reducing her home to ashes.

" 'Twould be an act worthy of cowardly curs like you," Mrs. Bates is said to have replied. "You may burn my house but my tongue will never stop as long as there's breath in my body."

One of the "Refugees" decided to find out about that. Seizing a firebrand he applied it to the Bates farmhouse. With quick action the widow had the fire out with a sudden slosh of water while her boys hurled a volley of stones at the enemy. Quickly the children were held fast and their mother was roped to a tree. From there the family was compelled to watch the house burn to the ground. Mulliner's gang waited until all was smoking ruin and then freed Widow Bates, departing with their booty.

It was soon evident that Joe himself did not approve of the escapade. After the story had spread through the countryside, neighbors assembled for a bee during which a new home was built, with donations of furniture and food contributed from many of the lost villages.

Mulliner himself provided the final gesture. Three hundred dollars suddenly appeared where it had not been before and it was always believed that Joe had taken this means to atone for the raid his gang made without orders.

Then there is the story of Quaker Bridge. Here today you'll find the poles and refuse of a deer-hunter's camp on the site of the old hotel which was a regular stage stop. The bridge for which the town was named was an old precarious structure, its baseboards fitted together with wooden pegs. Under the span passed the cedar waters of the Batsto River, making its way from Batsto to Hampton Gate and White Horse. Now a new span has been built to replace the historic structure, recently destroyed in a forest fire.

The original bridge was built by Quakers on their way to annual meeting in Tuckerton. In fording the stream, two or three members of the party were lost each year. Finally, the span was completed to forestall the loss of life which, until then, had been accepted with peculiar complacency.

Herds of deer scramble through the woods and along the winding uncertain paths of Quaker Bridge. There is nothing to show that here, years ago, was a hotel and one or two dwellings. And there is nothing to prove or disprove the story of Joe Mulliner's adventure.

It was a stormy night and dark when Joe suddenly appeared, his countenance radiant with rain and his smile revealing two rows of perfect teeth. As someone gasped, "Joe Mulliner!" the fiddler stopped and the dancers, moving in the dim-lit parlor of the inn, shuffled uncertainly. Mulliner instantly made a demand that the music go on and that the best-looking girl step out to dance with him.

It was an old demand and dancers of all the old towns and their stage-stop hotels were used to it. But though buxom damsels afterward boasted a dance with Mulliner they never willingly answered his invitations. On this occasion there was considerable reluctance. Swains held their girls tight and then Mulliner, whipping out his shooting-iron, gave the men a minute to disappear.

It is a story that has been worn with much handling but not yet has it been called a fable. A timid dancer, a chap perhaps who had been trying for many years to get up the nerve to dance, stayed in the room and defied the gang leader.

"My, my," laughed Mulliner, surprised. "And have all the bold fellows vanished, have all the hawks fled to cover, leaving this chicken-hearted fool among the wenches?"

He of the alleged chicken heart dropped the hand of his partner and swung his own flatly across the face of the intruder. Instead of firing, Mulliner laughed long and loud. Then he shook hands, declaring that so fearless "a little bantam" must have the best girl present. And taking the slapper's partner, he danced a round or two and vanished into the night.

At old Washington, not far beyond, the ruins of the inn

can still be found. The outline of the building, traced by
the stones in the long grass, shows it to have been one of
unusual size. Washington was a main stop and its inn must
have held many rooms.

In the depths of its cellar we found the carcass of a doe.
The deer had either broken its neck in the plunge or had
been shot by some hunter who intended to come back when
the wardens left the woods.

Old Washington, with the foundations of many buildings above the ground still showing and with a forgotten
pear orchard in bloom, is the locale of another Mulliner
story. A couple, not so loving apparently as they should
have been, arrived by stage at the tavern where the wedding
was to take place amid much jollification. An ox was
sizzling on the fire, women of the party were moving about
in rustling silk and the barkeep was passing out too many
draughts of ale—when Joe Mulliner arrived.

Mulliner, it seems, had come in by his favorite route, the
back door. Passing through the trees he came upon a girl,
pretty and dark, prone upon the grass, weeping. He stood
watching her a moment and then, quietly and with a concerned expression, he asked her what was wrong. For
answer, she looked up, and seeing a strange giant of a man,
fled into the inn.

Mulliner must have hung about the neighborhood until
the wedding itself was in progress. Then he suddenly appeared on the staircase overlooking the ceremony. From
there he saw that the girl being wed and the girl he had seen
behind the tavern were one and the same. His interest increased. Then he looked upon the groom and in doing so
recognized an old enemy. He made no cry but waited
his time.

The wedding ceremony went on. The moment came for the girl to say, "I do." The reply was slow and even then a wavering uncertainty. It was a reply, however, that was suddenly punctuated by a shot. The light providing most of the illumination was shattered. From the shadow of the stairs Joe Mulliner ordered the groom to leave the tavern. Seeing the glint of his gun, the stranger did as he was told. He did more: he left the wedding, the scene, and the story.

Perhaps the girl was pleased. Or perhaps, like those of her sex and age, she didn't know whether she was pleased or not, after the thing was done. But Mulliner, it is whispered, danced with her, imbibed more ale than was good for him, and returned to his gang.

It was a love of dancing and good company that spelled disaster and death for Joe Mulliner. With the depredations of his refugees dealing terror to South Jersey, men of the vicinity organized a company of rangers giving command to a Captain Baylin, an old Indian fighter, who swore he'd get Mulliner and all his crew. Joe, however, led the posse a merry chase long after that.

Then one night, Mulliner, longing for company other than his gang, boldly appeared at New Columbia, later Nescochague and now Nesco, where he danced with nimble step among the best of the party. One of the men at the inn, however, slipped out and through the lines of the Mulliner watchers. Word was sent to Captain Baylin and in no time the building was surrounded. Joe Mulliner, for the first time in his life, became a prisoner.

Under arrest he was taken to Woodbury (or Burlington), where he was charged with banditry and treason. Conviction and sentence to the gallows followed shortly after. While awaiting execution Joe was visited by two Methodist preachers of Colonial days, Cromwell and Petticord. Mulliner thanked them for their interest and according to the tale, made a fancy speech about the right way being the safe way. We choose to believe that Mulliner died as he lived, unafraid of death and polite to all who cared to associate with him. He was hanged, the legend goes, down on the buttonwoods of the shore road. More likely is the story that he was strung up officially at Woodbury gaol.

Captain Baylin pursued the remaining Refugees and after a sharp fight at the Hemlock Swamp, brought them to bay. Among those who did not escape was an army deserter, who, it is known, was hanged at Crowley's Point. But it makes a better ghost story, you see, to have Joe Mulliner breathe his last in that locality.

The outlaw's grave, marked now by a plain sign that surmounts the old stone, bears the inscription, "Joseph Mulliner, 1781." It was recently provided for the Indian King Fish and Hunt Club by Charles Dietz, of Audubon, a sign-painter. Long after the new sign has faded and crumbled away, the story of Joe Mulliner and of the forgotten towns he loved will be told and retold.

XXIII

HARRISIA OR HARRISVILLE

On sunny days, now that the new State road to New Gretna and the shore conquers the swamps and barrens down Speedwell way, motorists slow down as they come upon a forgotten village whose ruins resemble an ancient Roman aqueduct.

Where the Hospitality Creek, the Wading River, and the Oswego Branch close in for a meander to the sea, Harrisville, or Harrisia of more prosperous times, reminds an age of speed that here in the lonely woodlands was once a town built by another early industry, paper-making.

Forge and furnace towns have retained their normal identities through such colorful appellations as Mary Ann Forge, Hanover Furnace and Hampton Gate. Sawmill towns of long ago were similarly identified as Lower Mill, Upper Mill, Little Pine Mill or Webb Mill.

Too many names of the pinelands were bestowed by their owners in honor of themselves or by railroad officials who thought Chatsworth better than Chamong or Chesilhurst, Penbryn and Whiting more pleasant to pronounce than Aserdaten and Horicon.

Harrisville seems to trace its present and former names to the man who founded the paper mill, Richard Harris. After the town had been swept by a disastrous fire that frustrated any further attempts to carry on, Harris lived there, it is said, in voluntary exile. In later years he grew unusually stout so that his size was remarked on by all who knew him. Relatives came for him one day, took him to Philadelphia and there he died.

Harrisia, we were told by E. L. Jordan, of Atlantic City, was first of all McCartysville. Later the four Harris brothers took charge. William took care of the Philadelphia store, supplied by the plant. Ben and William were in charge of a store in New York at 55 Beekman Street. Richard and Howard lived in Harrisia.

The Harris homes were commodious affairs, Richard's being the largest. Richard seems to have been the wealthiest and director of the enterprise. His house, at the entrance of the little town, once a garden spot in Southern Jersey, commanded a view of the main street, lined with its gas lights, fueled, as were the houses, from a subterranean gas house across the road, where apparently gas was made from oil.

Richard was a particular man and demanded, above all things, definite, unyielding neatness. If, upon rising in the morning, he noted that a gate in front of some resident's home was ajar, he berated the owner, telling him that in the future he must surely be more careful.

There was a combined church and school as well as a store. Innumerable tenant houses stood at the other end of the village. A canal, leading from a lake fed by the Oswego Branch above the town, wound its way back of the houses and twisted through the plant, providing water power.

In the larger of the ruins today, one can find the remains of large frame moss-grown tubs. These were the vats in which black hay was boiled for the making of paper. The process was a secret one, they told us, and was stolen before a patent had been granted.

Ruins of the paper mill at Harrisville, perhaps the largest in New Jersey in the last century. Twisting through town and mill are the remains of intricate canal works dug to supply water power for the processing of salt hay into heavy paper and boards.

The last old house at Mary Ann Forge, opened about 1827 and closed in the '80's

The product was a thick brown paper which was finished outside the boiler buildings in large drying sheds. The buildings immediately around the boiler plant often caught on fire, for the smokepipe was unscreened.

Opposite the Richard Harris mansion, in which there were eleven large rooms, and near this favorite haunt of Henry Carey, was a grist mill. The building, from which the keystone had been stolen when we first pressed through, was burned before the fire swept the town out of existence Mrs. Jennie Risley, a daughter of Howard Harris, who hadn't seen her birthplace in more than forty years, lived in Port Republic. Jordan located her, after a long search, just a few months ago.

In Harrisia, home and garden privileges went with residence. Rent was free, if you worked in the plant, Mrs. Risley said. In time of sickness or death, horses and vehicles of the owner were at the disposal of all. There was free ice. Working hours were from 6 A. M. to 6 P. M. The mill force was assembled and dismissed by the ringing of a bell which has since been carried away. Wages were standard at a dollar and a quarter a day.

Richard Sooy, a cutter at the plant, hung on in Washington after the town was destroyed, this town from which he had walked back and forth through the scrubby woods every night and morning. From then on Sooy walked to old Pleasant Mills, moving his home eventually to Batsto. Once he trudged to the Pleasant Mills paper plant on time despite the fact that a blizzard was raging through the barrens. But the effort was too much: a few moments later he was found dead in the engine room.

Jordan now owns some of the felts from the Harrisia mill to remind him of the vanished town, founded, so far as we know, when Howard Harris married old McCarty's daughter, changing the name of the village and nearly everything else. Mail, sent to Harrisville once upon a time, went by mule team and boat along Wading River. Send a letter to Harrisville today and you'll probably get it back.

Harrisia, or Harrisville, remained all but forgotten until Emilio Carranza's plane, flying from New York to Washington, plunged headlong into the pines, from the rolling, bulging black of a thunderstorm. When news that the Mexican Good Will Flier's broken ship had been found was received from a berry-picker, thousands of persons began scanning their maps to discern the wild tangle to which another tragedy of the air had given fame. Carranza fell near Harris, a tiny station on the Jersey Central, ten miles from Harrisville. Harris was Harrisville's loading station and once the scene of industrial activity.

The first story of Harrisville gives it notice as a slitting mill in the year 1795. Slitting was a part of the early lumber operations. This slitting process is the earliest known method for reducing lumber to commercial sizes. Slitting was a splitting of the logs by use of mauls and wedges. Only the best timber, free from knots, could be used. That the slitting mill idea was not an outstanding success is shown in the fact that this mill at Harrisia seems to have been the only one of its kind, in the pinelands, that went on for any length of time.

Of course, there were many other lumber mills, cutting timber and making shingles as well as plaster lath. But these used a method of riving instead of slitting, using timber but four feet in length. Once in a while an old house is found somewhere in this pine country on which such shingles and lath were used. They are discovered so seldom, however, that they are usually pointed out as curiosities.

The transition of the old slitting mill into a paper plant seems to have occurred about 1815 here at Harrisia. The establishment took the name of the New York Machine Manufacturing Company, with power furnished from the Wading River Canal Manufacturing Company. The water power was provided by damming the Wading River and sluicing through a canal to the plant.

The size of the plant and the town that grew up around it cannot be surmised merely from the ruins as they jut into the sky today. There are many acres of scattered walls, the remains of two-story buildings, skeletons of a dead community. The main buildings are constructed entirely of Jersey stone and have walls two feet thick. Trimmings are of brick.

The stone is of a kind unknown in the immediate vicinity and must have been carried overland or possibly floated to the site on barges. The bricks must have been shipped from England, through Tuckerton as a port of entry. Both stone and brick were placed in position with lime mortar. Cement was unknown when these buildings were erected. The stone, brick, and lime are in a remarkable state of preservation, considering that it was back in 1893 that the town was swept by fire.

Once a fire started in Harrisia, there was no stopping it. It was the same then as it might be even now. Off there are the ends of a road that winds and bumps through thickets and over burned and fallen logs. No fire apparatus, no matter how intrepid its crew, could reach the town then. The conflagration that ended the paper town made a thorough job of it.

In what was unquestionably the key building, there is a

space from which some passer-by must have removed a name stone which possibly dated the start of the plant and described its business. The wild scraping vines are creeping over the aperture. That building that is circular has no windows. An iron pipe stabs through its wall and there is a drop of five feet to where, inside, the weeds have woven a carpet.

There is no machinery in the roofless structure. In some there are deep, shuddering pools of water. In others there are tumbled stones, broken bricks and the same awesome silence. Around the cluster of ruins the years have thrown a screen of beautiful cedars, trees that are symmetrical and highly decorative to the fire-stunted landscape.

Around and through the town is a labyrinth of the old canals and strange underground passages. Most of the canals are empty, but at their bottom is a mass of stones and broken brick swirled there through the sluiceways of the active years. Across the way from the tumbled buildings are gateposts that must have stood in front of an old house. Where the house was is just a yawning hole. Back from here there are the gnarled and twisted trees of an old apple orchard. Through them the uncertain road winds away toward Martha and Calico.

The Harrisia mill made paper, not from the wood pulp that might have been taken from the surrounding timberland, but from hay, as well as from rags, rope and waste paper shipped from New York and Philadelphia by languorous means. Loads of raw materials as well as the finished product were carted by mule teams to and from the principal shipping centers, and then, years later, to Harris Station.

It was a long, tedious haul to Harris, ten miles of a narrow one-way road. The lane was sandy, but its spots of shade lightened the long, crazy monotony. At places along the road there were passage points. There had to be a schedule for the teams traveled in caravans.

There was a too momentary flurry, recently, when it was noted in the news that George Thomas, fire warden and husband of the postmistress at Jenkins Neck, had died while fighting a fire near Harrisville. Thomas was one of the best-known residents of the vicinity. His memories went back with those of Willis Buzby to the past days of the pine towns. Thomas was perhaps the only one who had any authentic information on what happened when Harrisville ended its colorful career.

Thomas could remember that when he was a boy the mill was still in full operation, giving employment to many hands. He said he could remember the tall impressive build-ings of the plant and the houses around the orchard where the workers lived. He could remember Main Street, if that was its name, still marked by a fire-singed row of stately maples. This was the street, according to Thomas, that was illuminated by gas lights on ornamental iron uprights.

One of the strangest things about Harrisia is that in the center of town there is an Artesian well which flows con-tinually, filling the pools here and there and eventually creeping through the ruins and marshes to Wading River. The nine-inch driven pipe is rusted and breaking off. The water has a strong taste of iron. According to Thomas, the value of the paper plant was at one time definitely set at $700,000, a large figure in those days.

The canals which supplied the water power for the mill were dug in 1815, Thomas was certain. The diggings were made by contract along with the excavations for the plant at three cents a cubic yard. Labor then, Thomas recalled, could be had at nine cents per hour.

In his book on the vegetation of the New Jersey pine barrens, Professor John W. Harshberger lists as industries of the area the following: Lumbering, the making of turpentine, cranberry culture, peat digging, huckleberry picking, drug product cultivation and the gathering of greens and flowers. There seems to be no mention of the bog ore furnaces or the paper plants, but possibly they did not come in the professor's province.

Paper making was carried on here at Harrisia and at Pleasant Mills, at least, but along with the forges, it has been a forgotten business for a long, long time.

The new State highway, cutting through Chatsworth, pushing on to Speedwell and cutting through the brush with modern equipment of the road builder, goes on beyond the edge of the Oswego Branch near the Harrisia bridge. Now that the road has been completed, many of the secrets of the pinelands are being revealed to hundreds who have heard them in only occasional whispers. The heavy silence of the barrens echoes and re-echoes with the hum of motorcars and cries of town seekers who trace our trails. But Harrisia, the men who built it, and the minds who directed its construction and operation, are merged in the enigma that hems in the pinelands of Southern New Jersey.

XXIV

SKELETONS AND GLASS: UPPER MILL

A Cat that has nine lives to live
Can play a noble part;
A man with seven wives to please
Is beaten from the start.

ONCE upon a time, when the pine villages were important
centers in the new world, there was a town among them
called Upper Mill. The houses stood in a cluster on the
hill, grouped around a wayside tavern. Every night, when
tankards were filled, the drovers sang a song or two.

One particular ballad, we were told, concerned a cat that
had nine lives and a man who had seven wives. This little
tune was given a special gusto by a chap recalled as Bill
Hibben. Nobody knew just when it was that Bill had
come to Upper Mill or what had been his vocation before
he came. Some said he was a tramp, and the others didn't
care.

Bill, says the legend, had a good voice, a voice that was
at its very best in that lyric of the cat and numerous wives,
perhaps similar to the one we have reconstructed. Everybody knew why Bill liked that song; everybody knew that
his singing was given a more than ordinary fervor by the
token of personal experience. Bill had had seven wives.

Those were the days when life in the woods was casual,
when men lived for today and worried little about the
morrow. Days of easy marriages and quickly forgotten
weddings are not as modern as you were thinking, perhaps.

Those were the times when Old Squire Joyce held sway. Squire Joyce would perform a marriage for anybody for a dollar, with no questions asked. It made no difference if there was another wife. Nor would it cause comment even if the Squire knew all about such an additional spouse, through his having officiated at the previous ceremony.

If a man had tired of his consort, he could say so and get from the squire what that official called "clearance papers." These, said he, were as good as a divorce.

Charley Rogers, lone resident in Upper Mill when we were there, remembered Joyce and also Bill Hibben. Thin, smiling, freckled and tattooed, Charley, with a decided British accent, said he wouldn't swear to all the stories they have told about this pair. He merely chuckled in noncommittal acquiescence.

"Are you an Englishman?" we asked Charley.

"Well, I have been, part of the time," said Charley, smiling.

That's the way they answer questions in Upper Mill.

There is one more weird story to be retold about Bill Hibben before we leave him. Once, when one of his wives died, they couldn't locate Bill. They picked out a small clearing in the woods that seemed suitable for this one, Kate, a sort of potter's field. There they buried her. When Bill came back, he wasn't at all satisfied that Kate should lie in a lonely spot like that. Although it was a long time after the obsequies and the original burial had been made with but a box for a coffin, Bill, in spite of these facts, had the body exhumed and reburied in Brown's Mills.

Upper Mill, named for the mill that once stood beside a little stream that flows through its cranberry bog, Mac-Donald's Branch, was originally a stop-over for cattle drovers, rolling along on their way to Perth Amboy and New York. Thirty years ago there were but three houses. Now there is only one of those that formed the original village. It adjoins Rogers' home.

The oldest house was a small log cabin, just two hundred and sixteen years old. On one of the logs on the side is cut the inscription "Built in 1720." William H. Reeves, former Burlington County clerk and an authority on the history of the pinelands, says that there is no doubt of the date's authenticity.

Reeves, who owns a great deal of land in the vicinity, has a deed which refers to a Bispham Mill, which was apparently on the same site in the late 1600s. The grant refers to one Elizabeth Fenton, who controlled the property through most of the Seventeenth Century.

Rogers, who was sixty-five, remembers that Michael Mingin, who lived at the mill long ago, said that the carved date was authentic. Michael was then eighty-four and the year was 1910.

On one side of the building is a hole, four by twelve inches, five feet up from the ground. This, Rogers says, was a lookout and a vantage point from which besieged occupants could shoot at Indians. Rogers has found many Indian relics in the woods and clearings. Over the door of his home is an ancient Indian pony shoe.

The cabin and house adjoining grace the rise of a sandy knoll. Farther down the lane is the ruin of another house. Once, Rogers recalls, a visitor who came poking in the dirt serving as the floor of the cabin, dug up a pair of fine andirons. Back toward the woods there is a weather-beaten double house, its timbers rotting and its interior occupied by buzzing wasps and other insects. In its boards are the old square nails. On the cabin door is a hickory hinge, one of the few that remain in this section.

The land including Upper Mill is owned by Henry M. Black, of Jobstown, who operates several cranberry plantations. Below the dam used for flooding the Upper Mill is a cedar swamp. Large cedars and giant pines are seen with their tops pointing skyward far above the maples, gums and other more ordinary trees. It was over this swamp that Reeves says he saw the Sikorsky airplane of New England, which strangely vanished. Despite large rewards, no trace or word of the missing ship or its two passengers has ever been found.

It may be that the swamp at Upper Mill guards well the mystery of another air tragedy. The pines have many secrets and keep them all.

Not far from Upper Mill as the crow flies, but a considerable distance as an automobile must travel, over a bumping, winding trail through Reeves' bogs, is a clearing where the sun is reflected from many shining particles among the scrub. This is Lebanon, or Glass House, as the signboards call it, a forgotten glass-making village of Burlington County, now site of a CCC camp.

Except on very old maps, Lebanon makes no appearance. However, the town was of no little importance in its day. Located near the Eastern boundary of the county in Woodland Township, its heyday seems to have been definitely concluded by 1870.

Old Taylor Wainright (pronounced Wineright by pineland natives), a Civil War veteran of Brown's Mills, is one of the few who remembers the Lebanon glassworks in operation. Taylor is in his late eighties, hale, hearty and

A small log cabin at Upper Mill, bearing the inscription "Built in 1720," was still standing in the thirties. A lone last resident of the village was Charley Rogers (left).

Site of the old glass-making village of Lebanon, or Glass House, which made window panes, fancy bottles, and glass walking canes in the mid-nineteenth century. Now a part of the Lebanon State Forest.

clear of mind. He recalls that in 1861 when he marched away to answer the call of the colors, Lebanon's plant was buzzing with activity. The glassworks made windowpanes, for the most part, he told us. But they also turned out fancy bottles and glass walking-canes.

The soil at Lebanon is what is classified as shallow phase. For miles there is blinding white sand in the clearings between the trees. Then, just off the trail, in a cluster of cedars for which the town was named, the last of Lebanon can be seen in the glass-strewn ground, the ruins of old kilns and bricks from the factory buildings.

The product was hauled to Lumberton by cart, by way of Brown's Mills, Taylor informed us. The decorative articles were specialties, made for fun as it were, and not generally sold. Thomas Early, an old resident of Pemberton, recalls that as a young man he went to Lebanon, saw the plant in operation, and obtained from a workman some specimens of the town's product. These have been in Early's possession since about 1865.

According to Wainright's recollections, there were about twenty houses in Lebanon, prior to 1861. At least two hundred people, he says, must have been employed as woodmen, teamsters, sand-diggers and glass-blowers. One of the leading blowers and "pattern-men" was Mahlon Joslin, who died near by not so many years ago.

There is but one building on the property now, and that is down the lane from the village proper. This is the shanty of Victor Bush, of Turkeytown, better known as Magnolia.

"Vic," as he will tell you himself, never "had much schoolin' " and very little "bringin' up" as far as the final polishing goes, but in spite of that he has gone far in the confines of the woodland area in which he has lived his life.

He has served as a member of the Pemberton Township board of education. In addition he was elected to a term that stretched to many years on the Township Committee, which is the municipal governing body.

Bush had been for many years a forester with the New Jersey Department of Conservation and Development, whose chief purpose is to purchase and maintain forest and timber lands in various areas of the State. One of the largest and best known is the Lebanon State Forest, the wild woodland which now surrounds the old glass-making town. Here it is that Bush did his chief work. Among his duties were the prevention of fires, the removing of brush and superfluous branches of trees, in addition to the planting of seedlings. Experiments go on year after year to determine just what trees grow best in each particular kind of soil.

How curious it is to remember that just as one of Upper Mill's best stories concerns a cemetery, so does a narrative of Lebanon. Here, near the village, was once a graveyard, now all but obliterated because the many fires that sweep the section have destroyed headboards and rude wooden crosses. People have to die, and at Lebanon the necessity wasn't softened by the ministrations of the clergy.

There was no church and consequently, there was no preacher. However, there were workers in the glass plant known to have their more religious moments. One of these was always chosen to say the few kind words that launched the departed on his last, long journey. The grave was sometimes marked by a stone, but inasmuch as stones were few in this vicinity, a wooden marker was more commonly erected.

A few years ago, one of Bush's employes, William Martin, was known to have his superstitions. These included all lingering near graveyards, day or night. Telling Martin that his fears were foolish, Bush offered him five dollars to dig up a human body by moonlight. Bush said later that he never thought for a moment that Martin would do any digging or he would have recalled the offer.

The next night, when Bush was attending a gathering at a town ten miles away, there came a knock on the door. A woman answered the summons. With a scream, she fell back in a dead faint. Bush and his friends investigated quickly and most of them ran from the sight they beheld at the open aperture. Martin was on the stoop, a little bedraggled from his journey, and with a skeleton clasped in his arms!

Bush told Warner Hargrove that he was naturally in a quandary what to do. He consulted a coroner about what disposition he should make of the bones. The official advised him and charged thirty dollars for his recommendations. After that Bush had to give Martin his five dollars or face the prospect of having him shout the story all over the State. From that day to this Bush has given no dares, even on sure-fire wagers.

Thomas Shreve, of Pemberton, thoroughly familiar with old Upper Mill, Lebanon, and the lands that surround them, told us that at least twenty bodies were buried in the glass town's little cemetery. There isn't even a ghost story there today. Perhaps that is because there's no one left to tell any —not even the angry wraith of the fellow whose slumber Martin disturbed in order to earn his five dollars.

The Presbyterian church at Fairfield (Fairton), near New England Cross-

XXV

FAIRFIELD: FAIRTON: NEW ENGLAND CROSSROADS

Down on the bustling road that runs from Bridgeton to Cedarville's tree-canopied white houses, there is a little brown church. Around its white-shuttered mien of ancient dignity sleep the founders of a town of long ago, a town that with the exception of a scattering of farms, has moved on down the highway. This is the Old Stone Church of Fairfield, shrine and relic of the village New England Town.

The church is authentically old. The hundred and fiftieth anniversary of its building was celebrated only a few years ago. On that occasion, dignitaries of the Presbyterian Church gathered to pay homage to those pioneers who settled in this section of West New Jersey some time before 1692. There were two earlier churches further down the road toward Fairton, once Fairfield and later New England Town Cross Roads.

The village and its first church were on the south bank of the Cohansey River, which was once called Caesarea from New Jersey's earliest name, Nova Caesarea. The first minister there was Rev. Thomas Bridge, of Hackney, England. Mr. Bridge, in 1692, obtained, in return for his settling in the new land, a deed for one thousand acres wherever he wished to locate. An emissary of the West Jersey Society in England, he chose the cross-trails that were to become

Fairfield, not far from the bay, yet not too far inland for safety.

The whole section here goes back to an emigration of settlers who on April 16, 1696, appointed a group of representatives to convey from the owner, John Bellers, of London, a tract of five thousand acres. The newcomers traveled from New England, particularly Connecticut and Long Island, naming their new location Fairfield after Fairfield in Connecticut. Travel may have been slow and fraught with hardship in those days but within the year the Colonists were definitely established on the scene, plotting streets and building homes. The group was quaintly described as being "late of New England but now of Caesarea River, alias Cohansey."

Near the site of the first church there is a grove of tall oaks and cedars. To the experienced seeker of forgotten villages and evidence concerning people who lived in them, the presence of cedars in any sort of symmetry nearly always points to the presence of an old graveyard. On the Mullica, a grove of cedars is all that marks the burying-ground of the early Swedes. On the Cohansey these first two churches have gone but their members slumber 'neath the evergreen trees.

Beside the woods on a little knoll, the exact location of the meeting houses, is a monument erected twenty odd years ago. It is in memory of "the true and good men and women, who, coming in the Seventeenth Century, founded here on the Cohansey the Church of Christ in Fairfield." This church did not come under the charge of the Presbytery until 1708.

Of all the cemeteries in South Jersey you will perhaps find this one of the most curious. It is a necessity, first of all, to look for the stones. They will be found, here and there, through the grove beneath a growth of scrub oak that in many cases conceals them entirely. Many of the trees were planted to mark the head and foot of those who were interred. The trees have now bowled the stones awry.

There are some who hold that rummaging in cemeteries is morbid business. Such is seldom the case. On tombstones in old graveyards is traced the history of pioneers who put down foundations for a nation's hope of freedom. Where else, except perhaps beside the Old Stone Church, is there anything to tell of the existence of New England Town and Fairfield, let alone "the hopes and fears of all the years"?

Here is the stone of one Israel Petty "Junr" who at thirty-four died in 1763. Under another hidden marker "lyes" the body of Thomas Harris, who died in 1759. Other graves are those of Ruth, wife of Capt. David Page, 1777. (David seems to lie nowhere in the vicinity. Perhaps as a follower of the sea he was lost with his ship.) Among the others who died before a new nation progressed very far are Jeremiah Nixon, 1766; Hon. Theophilus Elmer, "who took leave of time" in 1783; David Fithian, 1754; Richard Powel, 1764; Benjamin Parvin, 1755; another Parvin, 1743, and Thomas Alling, whose 1761 is written "J76J," resembling a telephone number.

A giant tree has almost entirely obscured the inscription on the leaning stone of Mariah Clun, 1777. Sarah Smith's vault is inscribed with these words: "Here lies deposited the body of Sarah Smith, successively the wife of the Rev. William Ramsay, of this place, and the Rev. Dr. Robert Smith" who was "highly distinguished for the exercise of the humble and amiable qualities in her relations as wife, mother, friend, and Christian."

Beside Sarah's grave is that of her first husband, its inscription unreadable. The Rev. Mr. Ramsay was pastor of the church from 1756 to 1771, in which year he died. We wondered, in passing, where Dr. Smith served and where, at the last, they buried him. Further on toward the river are the graves of Lois and Nathaniel Diameter; James Boyd, a Philadelphia merchant; Rhodha, wife of Henry Sparks, and Ezekiel Wescote, pioneers all. Beside some of the stones a path has been worn as if by kin seeking their forbears. A wagon road meanders through the cloistered shade down to the Cohansey whose waters brought many a funeral barge to this very shore in those early years.

Returning up the roadway to the Old Stone Church, one must pass by the road that wanders down to Sea Breeze, now a tiny bay resort with a hotel built on the site of one that burned years ago, and never occupied since its completion. Things have been postponed here, natives will tell you, because telephones and electricity have not been carried through. Several small cabins fringe the bay shore. If you pass the William Buck brick farmhouse, dated 1781, you will know you are on the right road. If you come upon an unkempt little house where a group of untidy children say a listless "I don't know" in response to all your questions, you have lost your way.

The Old Stone Church is in an excellent state of preservation in spite of care which, to say the least, seems to be casual enough. The key to the place may be obtained by almost anybody at J. H. Livingston's store in Fairton. Here, too, one can procure rather good snapshots of the church's exterior and interior, sold by Livingston to pay for the building's upkeep. The place is truly worthy of an attendant who could guard its treasures as well as tell its story to those who call.

The white doors swing back on their original hinges and at once the visitor is in a dry and musty interior, smelling of ancient woodwork. The doors are at the back and lead forward over an indoor brick pavement similar to those of an old street. The space under the stiff-backed pews, some gated, others arranged at a variety of angles to accommodate the throng that must have insisted on watching their preacher, is covered with wooden flooring. There is no cellar. From the middle of the two aisles two stoves once sent their pipes through the roof. Now there is but one inasmuch as services are held but once each year.

At the center is a pulpit, high enough to overlook the downstairs congregation and with a vantage from which every corner of the three-sided balcony may be seen, as well. To this lofty perch, overhung by a canopy, there is a small narrow stairs. Below is an enclosure from where the rest of the service would be conducted, elevated a little from benches of brown and white. Over the pulpit hangs the portrait of Rev. Ethan Osborn, who served the church as pastor for fifty-five years.

The grave of "Father Osborn," as he was called, is directly behind the church. It is marked with a formidable shaft which proclaims him a soldier of the Revolution, "a good man and a faithful minister of the Gospel." Father Osborn graduated from Dartmouth in 1784, was licensed to preach in 1786 and was called to Fairfield in 1788. He was ordained in 1789, resigned his charge in 1844 and died at the age of ninety-nine years eight months and ten days, "full of faith and in the hope of a joyful resurrection."

Father Osborn, born in Litchfield, Conn., journeyed from that town to Fairfield, on horseback. The congregation he was to serve was scattered all through the country now located in Fairfield, Deerfield and Downe Townships, a flock numbering, roughly, two thousand souls. These people were of Puritan origin and as Capt. Benjamin Brown Osborn, a grandson of the doughty preacher, has put it, "brought from the land of steady habits many of the manners and customs of New England. They were great churchgoers and they came trooping in, filling the seats below and the seats above, often running over into stairways and aisles."

The preacher was still active at ninety-seven when he preached his farewell sermon in the Fairfield Church. The congregation was distributed tightly in the lined pews, many had chairs in the aisles and many others were compelled to stand huddled by the doors. Father Osborn mounted to his pulpit, unassisted. When he concluded he came down with a look of triumph, as if he had closed some valiant chapter of his life. He had closed the book of a church's service, as well, but he did not know it then.

On the desk under the pulpit there are two registry books for visitors. The names inscribed go back for many years and number among them many descendants of the famous minister, one of whom, we were told, is now a rector in Georgia. Against the books is an old-fashioned collection box with its long handle. In the cupboard, a gloomy, cobwebby hovel behind the desk are several more, together with a funeral litter. Several stools are labelled to indicate the names of families who used them.

Under Father Osborn's portrait is the facsimile of a letter, signed by one hundred and five members of the congregation, which called the minister to serve the Fairfield Church. We quote from a few of its paragraphs, using the original spelling:

Mr. Ethan Ozburn—Sir: We the subscribing members of the Prisbeterian congregation at Fairfield in the County of Cumberland and State of New Jersey, have been for some time passed destitute of the state means of grace, the preaching of the Word of God. We do most sincerely lement the loss of so great a blessing and desire to bewail our sins which has provoked the Lord to strip us of these privileges we have so long enjoyed and too much abused. Being deeply affected with this our bereaved situation we would most humbly implore the Supreme Ruler of All Events and Head of the Church so to dispose the hearts of this people that truly repenting of our sins and turning unto God he would most graciously return unto us and grant the settlement of the Gosple in this place again.

The call went on in detail to explain that, as pastor, Father Osborn would receive the use of the parsonage, one hundred and fifty acres of land, its house and buildings as well as "one hundred pounds per annum to be paid either in gold or silver." The letter concluded hoping the young man would "except this our call," under date of March 21, 1789.

Outside the church there are stones almost as unusual as in the other graveyard but we must not dwell on them. There are many like those from which the church was built, marking graves without inscription. Of the more unusual epitaphs one, declining to mention death by name, says that Mary Elmer, in 1804, "paid the debt due God and Nature." Another, apparently similarly motivated, says that "Rhoda, wife of Amos Wescott, Esq., took her exit out of time into Eternity."

There are at least two Revolutionary soldiers,—Amariah

Harris, who died in 1793, and Captain James Burch. Fayette Pierson, editor of the *West Jersey Observer* and *Bridgeton Aurora* before and during the Civil War, also lies here.

Among the Batemans, Shaws, Prestons, Wescotts and Newcombs in the iron-fenced inclosure, one relict greets all who pass with this eerie inscription:

> "Let worms devour my wasting flesh,
>   And crumble all my bones to dust;
> My God shall raise my frame afresh
>   At the revival of the just."

The sudden mingling of these people, those who had been Puritans seeking a new kind of freedom, and West Jersey colonists, resenting in some measure the intrusion, provided an atmosphere charged with all sorts of lightning. Each faction sought favor with the Royal Governors to its own advantage. Judges, justices and jurors were chosen through backstage manoeuvering. Devices and trickery, often looked upon as the modern legacy of politics, were employed in all forms during those early days. Illegal votes were counted. Legal ballots were thrown out if they weren't on the chosen side. Clamor of riots often disturbed the villages and their polling places.

Taxes were burdensome. In the regime of Lord Cornbury, Governor since 1707, there had begun a period of oppression and bizarre cavortings of justice almost unimaginable. There was no more venomously hated man in the day than Cornbury, who answered protests against monopolies and restricted roads with paradings in women's apparel on the ramparts of the fort he called home. He was recalled after three years but the unrest he sowed lived long after his rule ceased.

Seventy years before the Revolution, which was the culmination of such shadowy practices, people of Fairfield and their neighbors made formal protest to the Crown and refused to pay a constable amounts which had been assessed.

Wee whose names are under written, [they wrote,] do utterlie denie to pay or to suffer to be taken by distress or any other ways any money, goods or any other thing by Francis Pagit, our so called constable because wee doubt of his being a lawful constable and more especially because we have been illegally assessed.

This case dragged through the courts for many years but finally, although indictments of the principals were returned, the matter petered out.

Roads of those early days were faint trails. There undoubtedly was one down to Delaware Bay where ships were moored and where fish could be procured when times were hard. It was not until 1756 that a stage line started between Philadelphia and New York, via Trenton; the trip required all of three days. In 1765 the stages, instead of leaving once a week, increased the schedule to two, but the speed remained about the same. Transportation, over land, from Cumberland County, was risky business and was undertaken by no organized means. Individuals and groups rode horseback, the same once reliable means employed by Father Osborn in his long ride from Connecticut.

The road question became a lottery problem in this vicinity during 1765 from which time, until 1768, attempts were made to raise funds for roads by lottery. Trails had become impassable. Many highways were becoming lost for lack of use. Mails, though they were fairly fast when they got through, were as much as two and three weeks behind.

Folk of Fairfield were in many ways self-sustaining. Mails and travelers cut them off from the world outside but they had prepared for that. From these villages near the shore, natives, during the war days, boiled out, dried and strung large quantities of clams which were sent by courier to the half-starved soldiery. It is reasonable to believe that such substitutes for beef and pork were sent from New England Cross Roads to Valley Forge. Commerce, such as it was, was carried over a road winding from Fairfield to Burlington, originally laid out in 1695.

They told us that Sarah Smith, who was the wife of the two ministers, was a lineal descendant of Swedish royalty. Her great-grandmother, Elizabeth, was compelled to flee her native country during an insurrection and found refuge in a hogshead concealed on board a vessel at Stockholm. The ship set sail, meanwhile, for America. Elizabeth brought many valued treasures with her, but lost them all when the vessel was wrecked on the Jersey shore. The lady, with members of the crew, managed to escape.

This picturesque ancestor of the minister's helpmeet was befriended in the wilderness of the Jersey shore by a wandering hunter whose name, it seems, was Garrison. Acquaintance became romance and later, even more. The couple were married. Ten children followed, the youngest of whom, William, was born in his mother's fifty-fifth year. A grandson, who lived in Bridgeton about seventy-five years ago, said that in his time his grandmother had more than a thousand living descendants in the country.

Among the more famous personages in the Old Stone Church yard is General Ebenezer Elmer, president of the

New Jersey Cincinnati Society and last surviving officer of the New Jersey line of the Revolutionary Army. General Elmer died in 1843 and was buried by Father Osborn, a compatriot at arms. The general was born in Cedarville and was a grandson of Rev. Daniel Elmer, one of the original settlers who had come from Fairfield, Conn. He was a brother of Dr. Jonathan Elmer, undertook the study of medicine and was about to practise when hostilities began with England. After serving during the war, he married and became a practising physician in Bridgeton, in former days known merely as The Bridge.

General Elmer served as a member and speaker of the Assembly, was a member of Congress under Jefferson in addition to serving as adjutant general of the Militia of New Jersey. During the War of 1812 he was in command of troops in Billingsport and later served as Collector of the Port of Bridgeton, which office he resigned in 1817. Later, in 1822, he was reappointed for another ten years. The inhabitants of Bridgeton and vicinity being firm backers of their country in the war for independence, a military corps was formed with General Joseph Bloomfield as captain and General Elmer as lieutenant. The corps joined the forces of General Schuyler, upon the conclusion of a long march.

During early days, when belief in witchcraft was prevalent and when the power of charms was admitted, such practices seem to have had a firm hold in the country of Fairfield and New England Town. It was customary for country folk to wear, hung about the neck, a piece of dried beef, cut in the shape of a heart with two needles inserted in the form of a cross. This was a protection against witches.

Mrs. Albert R. McAllister, wife of the Cumberland Senator, has in her home in Bridgeton a witch's ball which, hung in garrets of homes in the vicinity, was supposed to keep away evil spirits. The "H" and "L" hinges of Colonial cupboards and closets were also protective gadgets, guarding against ghosts and goblins and the like. The "H" stood for Holy and the "L" for Lord, as many must already know.

Another safeguard was a horseshoe, originally nailed boldly over doors and in prominent places, as they will still be found today. In this section "pow-wowing" was common. When persons were afflicted with fever or even a burn, others gifted with the special knowledge were called. Cure was supposed to follow the mumbling of Scriptural passages. The secrets of this strange business could not be imparted by the possessor except to a person of the opposite sex.

Among these early folk of Fairfield it was in some houses a bad omen to sweep one's rooms after sunset or to sweep dirt into the fire. These beliefs were probably imparted by the early Dutch. It was a safeguard, however, when using eggs, to sprinkle salt on their shells and cast them into the fire. Bread, it was claimed, could never be light unless a cross was made in the dough. Modern women, who make bread today, place a cross on the kneaded and floured dough, a habit that has been handed down, perhaps without explanation, by their mothers and grandmothers.

Such, then, is Fairfield's story. And as it has clicked to paper, it is as if someone were watching over it, silently approving, or, perhaps, withholding his disapproval.

XXVI

THE MURDER AT BAMBER

ON THE morning of September 15, 1884, James Wainwright, "a well-known, sober, honest and industrious laborer," left his home on the outskirts of the village of Toms River, to become one of the principals of a mystery which was to celebrate, at least temporarily, a tiny town now all but forgotten. Here at this wayside hamlet, five days later, Wainwright's body was found, all but submerged in the murky waters of a winding brook.

The discovery was a gruesome one. Wainwright's hand had broken free and was waving slowly back and forth above the surface. The village was Bamber and later Cedar Crest.

First notice of the story appeared in the Camden *Daily Courier* of September 20, 1884. Wainwright, "having a family of three sons, two daughters and a wife" left his home "to do a job of work for a neighbor. Before he had gone many yards from his door two reports from a shotgun were heard and the groans of a person."

Wainwright never returned and three days later, Toms River, a county seat which had boasted that an execution had never been carried out within its jurisdiction, was in the throes of gossip, hasty explanations and contradictory theories.

A searching party found Wainwright's pipe in a clump of bushes where the leaves seemed to have been disturbed by a tussle. A space where the ground had been clotted with blood was uncovered a few moments later.

"The excitement became intense," said the *Courier*, "and the crowd continuing to increase, the hunt went on with the fierceness of bloodhounds.

"There was evidence of the track of a body dragged through the underbrush. It led to the edge of a dismal swamp. One man uttered a loud cry and springing into the mire grasped what he thought to be the missing man's toe just sticking out of the mud. It proved to be his hat folded in and all buried but an inch of brim."

The hiding place of the corpse itself was the Bamber creek. The body had been floated up the stream to a bend where there was a deep pool. It had been weighted down by the slayer, who believed his crime would never be discovered.

In the first Press notice, it was revealed that two sons were strongly suspected, "while a prominent citizen of Toms River has been placed under a cloud owing to an intimacy that is charged to have existed between him and the murdered man's wife. This citizen," said the *Courier*, "is a candidate for Sheriff and has always been regarded as a consistent churchman. No arrests have yet been made. The Sheriff of the county has offered a reward of one hundred dollars."

That was on Saturday. On Monday, Elson H. Rockwell, the candidate for Sheriff, as well as all the members of Wainwright's family, were in custody. After a preliminary hearing before Squire Wilkes, it was brought out that the murder had been carefully and deliberately planned and that Wainwright had been shot within three hundred yards of his own door. The body had been temporarily concealed and then hauled away in a wagon. The clothing was then removed before the cadaver was plunged deep in the creek.

A theory suggested at the time was that Wainwright's eldest son had committed the murder, at the instigation of Rockwell.

Rockwell was forty-five. He had come to Toms River with his father and two brothers thirty years before. After a short residence there, he removed to New York where he entered the coal business. His leg was injured in a street-car accident and he sued the company, obtaining $13,000 damages. Twelve years before the murder, he returned to Toms River.

When he came back, it was in company with his wife and two children. In 1880 Mrs. Rockwell was taken ill, and Mrs. Wainwright, Julia by name, entered the picture. She nursed Mrs. Rockwell until she died and then continued to do Rockwell's housework and "mind his children." Wainwright, from the first, suspected undue intimacy between his wife and Rockwell. That he had excellent grounds for his suspicions was shown in later statements of a married daughter, Addie, and a son, Charles.

Finally, Mrs. Wainwright ceased to visit Rockwell's house openly. But, it was gossiped, the couple continued to meet clandestinely, to avert talk. A feud between the two men resulted in no time. Wainwright, it was testified, threatened to kill Rockwell.

Following a rather thorough autopsy, Wainwright was buried September 23rd. A brother who followed the cortège to the grave vowed he would see the murderer hanged. In this solemn declaration he was joined by members of the Grand Army of the Republic, who had just buried their comrade, as well as by prominent Democrats of Ocean County, associates of the former soldier.

A promise was made on the day of the funeral to produce as witness a man who had been courting one of Wainwright's daughters. This chap was said to have heard a family quarrel between Wainwright, and his son, George, which had all but terminated in blows. The murder followed next morning.

Prosecutor Middleton marshaled his evidence. Two camps formed, both Rockwell and Wainwright having large followings. The size of the wheels on Rockwell's wagon was found to correspond with the wagon track found near the bridge beyond which the body had been discovered. Dr. Schureman, the examiner, was uncertain, however, that spots on the bottom of the wagon were blood. Action was delayed, pending arrival of the Attorney General.

Evidence piled up against Rockwell. A fire in which Wainwright's clothes had been burned was found to have been kindled in pine needles, brought to the scene from some distance. Rockwell, met returning from Bamber with a load of fence rails, admitted he had also carried a pile of new-cut pine boughs. Rockwell, it was explained, was thoroughly familiar with the country about Bamber, having owned property there.

It was discovered Rockwell had been defeated in his run for Sheriff three years before because of the scandal caused by his association with Wainwright's wife, a story her husband had whispered abroad as much as he could.

William Beamer, one of the party discovering the body, said at the inquest that he had seen Rockwell at Bamber on the day of the crime and that "he looked sick." The dead man's widow created a sensation by appearing on the stand but she was mostly forgetful. Displaying no emotion at all, she could not remember when she had seen her husband last alive. She thought she had remained for the most part at the Magnolia Hotel that day, explaining her indifference to her husband's whereabouts by saying she had been told he had gone off to the beach. A daughter, Emma, proved to be a witness equally as difficult.

A surprising letter was received by Prosecutor Middleton from John Wainwright, an uncle of the victim, revealing a strange parallel to the crime. The writer recalled that a granduncle of Wainwright, a tax collector in Monmouth County, had been murdered in 1792 by two brothers, and that the body had been found similarly staked down, but in a roadside ditch.

The inquest dragged on. Amid the drone of nothings, Wilson, a Pinkerton detective with a bullet head and piercing eyes, took the stand. In a cold, decisive voice, this investigator declared that he had matched the slugs taken from Wainwright's body with remnants of some lead fishing sinkers found in a box on the mantle of Rockwell's home.

Jeff Thompson, still another witness, charged that on the day before the crime, George Wainwright sought to borrow his wagon and didn't get it. Emma Wainwright, recalled to the stand, said she would swear on a pile of Bibles as high as the Courthouse that her brothers didn't commit the murder, that her mother was equally guiltless and that "the man did it who carted the body away and nothing can ever change my mind."

A coroner's jury, after three hours, brought in the verdict

that James Wainwright had been murdered by one whose name was unknown, that he was "aided and abetted, counseled and procured" by E. K. Rockwell, Julia, Mary, Emma, George and Charlie Wainwright, and that the jurors "on their oath find that these defendants were there and then present, aiding and counseling the unknown man to commit the murder."

The accused were committed for the Grand Jury's action while Hooper Wainwright, the youngest son, and Thompson were discharged from custody. Indictment of Rockwell and the Wainwrights soon followed and long trial was begun January 21, 1885.

Prosecutor Middleton announced that George Wainwright had said, even before the finding of the body, that gunshot wounds would be discovered in the back and head of his father. All was excitement in Toms River as new entanglements presented themselves immediately.

The defense made a move to save Rockwell by showing that Thomas Lukes, who had given testimony about measurements of Rockwell's wagon, had ordered a new body put on his cart the day after the murder. Paint, which admittedly could have been from either Rockwell's or Lukes' wagon, was found rubbed off on the trees in a grove through which a vehicle had come, bearing its gruesome burden.

Rockwell's nephew, a law student, sat close to his uncle at the trial. Many of Mrs. Wainwright's relatives were present in the crowded court room but they would have nothing to do with her.

The trial dragged. An army of witnesses, producing conflicting and divergent testimony, trooped to and from the stand. Clayton Robbins, once sheriff of the county and the last witness to take the stand on January 23rd, interluded new details, charging that Rockwell, despite his advice, didn't seem anxious for an investigation. Coroner's helpers, lawyers, witnesses marched along. Interest lagged a little at times, except when Harvey Craft, postmaster at Bamber, told of intimacies of the murdered man's wife and Rockwell.

Rockwell's eyes frequently snapped at revelations which indexed the thoroughness of old-time sleuthing. He was particularly disturbed when a box from his home was offered in evidence, containing shot of various sizes. He was almost beside himself when a Captain Cook, proprietor of the Ocean Hotel, near which, it was said, the body of Wainwright had lain in the wagon all night, produced a telltale brass trousers button found near-by.

Mrs. Caroline Witzel, sworn February 3rd, told of hearing the shots which were supposed to have killed Wainwright. ("Wineright" is the way Ocean County folk pronounced it.) Counsellor Lindabury, questioning Mrs. Witzel, learned that after hearing the shots she had also remarked the barking of dogs and a voice screaming, "Oh, George, don't!"

This sudden sensation was interrupted by the anticlimax of an announcement that Edward Sherman, a hostler, conceded to be an important witness, had hanged himself in his barn, bereaving a wife and four children.

Evidence and more evidence filled volumes of testimony in the case. At last the *Courier*, tiring of printing half a column a day with short snatches of questions and answers, pulled the story down to two or three paragraphs appearing only every two or three days.

The defense began summing up on February 20th.

Lindabury, who had been invaluable as an aide to the prosecutor, sometimes referred to in the accounts as district attorney, rested for the state on February 26th. Judge Van Sickle directed the jury next day, to acquit Charles Wainwright and his two sisters but commended sentences· for the son, George, and Rockwell.

The jury, after deliberating a day and a night, found Rockwell guilty of second degree murder and acquitted George. Judge Van Sickle sentenced Rockwell to twenty years in State's prison. It was whispered at the time that if justice had been travestied in the conclusion of Ocean County's most sensational murder case, critics who said so should wait patiently and see what happened later. Rockwell was pardoned after serving seven years.

By a strange twist of Fate he spent his last years at Bamber. He built himself a cabin, the foundations of which can still be seen, less than a mile from the spot where the court said he concealed the body of the man he slew. Here, alone, with a secret of the case locked in his heart forever, he died, little more than thirty years ago. What became of his two children, the Wainwrights and the woman whose release he purchased at so bitter a price will be, for all time, part of the puzzle that is Bamber today.

Bamber is in that part of South Jersey in which to those familiar with its fastnesses, it is not strange that men and airplanes have been swallowed up. Bamber is the name upon the maps, but on its station is an intermediate title, one which was thought potent enough once to live down the old days—Cedar Crest. This is the name you will find on the deserted depot, its rusted signals and initialed waiting rooms tracing the passage of time and people.

A passenger on the old-fashioned, seldom-traveled

Tuckerton Railroad branch is an occasion. There is a one-room district school. But Charles Bunnell, who occupies one of the three or four inhabited dwellings near the station, is ever hopeful for business. He has built a refreshment stand for motorists who are curious enough to take a byway beyond the rolling plains, a short-cut to Forked River.

Back in the scrub behind Bunnell's house there are six or eight large, weather-swept but unoccupied houses, on a weed-grown and hardly discernible "Main Street," the last of the booming realty development and fruit farm at Cedar Crest.

Gullible enthusiastic souls, years ago, perceiving that the soil and conditions at Bamber were like those of Georgia, decided that here they would start a peach farm. Accordingly, as far as the eye can see, some nine hundred acres were planted with one hundred and thirty-five thousand trees. These trees are now scaly derelicts, prey of pests, wind, and weather, surrounded by stunted pines.

Up the road are ruins of what was a brick factory, once combined with a sawmill that manufactured excelsior. Down from the station is a loading shed on a broken siding, with bits of baskets left inside to show that for a few seasons, at least, the peach orchards yielded a crop. Down on a little crossroad, through a grove of trees where deer cross in the creepy solitude, is Bamber lake, a stretch of water that would do better justice to Maine. There are two old houses by the lakeside with signs of occupancy in deer season. Not so very long ago there was a camp for boys there.

Beside the lake is an old, decaying sawmill, a picturesque building, tumbling piece by piece into the rotting flume. The wheels will never turn again even though freshets drive the cedar water in frothy cascades. The lake laps against the wooden landing near the spillway, splashing toward where its eddies long ago revealed the shuddersome sight of a murder victim.

Gloucester Tavern, as it used to be, the center of attraction in a bustling iron town. From an old photograph found in the Little Red Farm.

XXVII

GLOUCESTER FURNACE

IN THE *History and Gazetteer of New Jersey*, published in in 1833, 103 years ago, there appears this notation:

GLOUCESTER, post-town and furnace of Galloway Township, Gloucester County, upon Landing Creek, a branch of the Mullica or Little Egg Harbor River, 36 miles S. E. from Woodbury, 71 from Trenton and 179 from W. C.; contains a furnace, grist and saw mill, a store, tavern and a number of dwellings, chiefly for the accommodation of workmen, of whom there are about 60, constantly employed, whose families may amount to 300 persons. The furnace makes annually about 800 tons of iron, chiefly castings, and has annexed to it about 25,000 acres of land.

That description, brief as it is, conjures up a picture of activity. One hears the ring of the saw in the mill, the wash of the wheel beside the stream as it rushes to the Mullica River. One sees many wagons on the road, many figures at work smelting bog ore. From far away come the mingled cries of children at school and the shouts of men who cast loose the moorings of a steamboat laden with village products.

To these details of imaginative remembering there must be compared the scene as one can find it today, across the road leading out of Egg Harbor City to Lower Bank and off to the right on a spur that goes through to Clark's Landing.

The site of the village is marked today by the unmistakable relics in the soil. Where the iron furnace stood is the dim outline of foundations, the residue slag assuming two long piles among the scraps of castings. Where the sawmill stood, there is a large amount of soggy sawdust. A burned portion of the sluiceway and a rusted water wheel are all that remain of the grist mill. After the history of 1833 was out, a glass works came into being, as well, for there are bits of Jersey glass along the bank of Landing Creek to prove its existence.

There is one house that is barred and locked and was no doubt occupied in summer. But beyond it, in a grove of trees, are four or five hollow shells that once were dwellings. Above the dam is a cranberry bog burned out in a fire that swept the vicinity some years ago. On every hand is quiet and slow-but-sure decay. It is difficult to understand that in these desolate surroundings was once a village humming with industries.

The tiny road that leads to Gloucester indicates clearly that there is little activity in this area now. One leaves the main road a mile or two beyond the Bungalow Hotel, back of which, beside two concrete bins, one may find the grave of a woman and her two children, who, in local legend, were scalped by Indians. The tiny cemetery has been enclosed by kindly hands and the graves, marked years ago by the planting of the customary cedar trees, are easily discovered in the woodland grove.

On the lone tombstone one may read the description: "Here lieth the mortal remains of Mrs. Sibbel Shaler, consort of Timothy Shaler, who died on the second day of April, 1783, in the 54th year of her life, with her two children." That is all the information the well-preserved stone imparts, but the story goes that Timothy, a sea captain, returned home to find his house burned and his wife and children slain in a raid by the Lenapes.

There are other stories subscribed to by John Edward Fisher, his wife and their five sons, who live in what was once known as "The Little Red Farm," reputed to be the first house of old Gloucester. The farm was so called in early deeds of the locality, many of which are held by the Fishers. The house was originally one room and was built by Conrad Marr, Fisher's grandfather, who came to Gloucester from Germany.

Fisher, who is 60, remembers many of the old legends as well as some of the scenes of actual activity in the village.

"Back across the road in the woods," he told us, "there are Indian graves. And did you see that tall oak tree beside the drive, as you came in? Lightning struck that tree years ago and some grape-shot from the Revolutionary War fell out."

The Fishers have the grape-shot among their other treasures and heirlooms. These include arrowheads, tomahawks, several old German Bibles and old coins. Among the coins, found in the fields and around the ruins of buildings that have disappeared, are an 1835 ten-cent piece, an 1809 half penny, an 1819 cartwheel, an 1864 two-cent piece and an 1872 five-cent piece.

"There was a bag of Spanish coins somewhere," Ray Fisher, formerly a Coast Guard, one of Fisher's sturdy sons, reminded his father "but somebody took that once."

That remark made Mrs. Fisher remember that another visitor had carried away a water-color sketch, made by one of Gloucester's pioneers, showing all the industrial plants as well as the Gloucester shot tower, beside the furnace where Revolutionary ammunition was made.

The failure of a narrow-gauge railroad to go through to Tuckerton is blamed, among other things, for Gloucester's dissolution. They got the track as far as Gloucester but then, according to the Fishers, Lower Bank refused to go through with its portion. The rails were torn up, subsequently, but from the Egg Harbor end first. As a result, three freight cars were stranded in the woods. They rotted and fell apart, through the years that followed.

"Why, this was a great town once," the elder Fisher recalled. "There were the mills and the foundry and a wagon-works, too, in addition to the glass factory. There was always something doing in town. The road was lined with houses, and full of wagons hauling goods down to the landing. There the steamboats would come, taking the goods down the Mullica, out through Great Bay and up to New York."

The "goods" included sewer pipes for Gotham streets.

The stream is narrowed down and walled in by tall marsh grass these days. Although it once saw "anything from a 25-footer up" near where you'll find the bridge, little more than a small motorboat could make it now. The houses and wharves last used by the salt hay market are rotting to pieces. The only sign of habitation here by the water is the tiny shack of a colored family. Near this point is the outline of foundations of the old hotel.

You get a queer feeling when you stand in a place such as this, realizing all that has vanished in dust in a mere century. Houses, factories, the hotel and school—as well as nearly all the people who knew them well—have disappeared.

XXVIII

CATAWBA AND ETNA

Less than 200 feet off the road that leads from Mays Landing to Ocean City, through English Creek, is a scattering of broken tombstones. Near-by, in the sandy soil, is the faintly traceable outline of a chapel. Through the trees, across a mucky swamp, are bricks and bits of Jersey stone, indicating that once there were a number of dwellings, huddled together in a small village.

This was Catawba. If mystery shrouds it now, a deeper mystery more than 100 years ago "hexed" it as a hollow shambles. Death, cunningly administered through a deadly poison, carried off five members of Catawba's principal family. Soon after, such survivors as there were moved away to escape the pall which had fallen on their town.

Information that Catawba's story was an arresting one came simultaneously from Jack Regensburg, of Haddonfield, and Donald Basenfelder, whose home was in English Creek. Thousands of motorists, they said, on their way to Ocean City and other near-by resorts of Atlantic and Cape May Counties, had sped by the spot, beyond Gravelly Run and close to the muddy banks of Miry Run, without knowing that once a community had begun prosperously here, only to be obliterated by what the legends say was a sinister plot.

On some of the older maps Catawba is well located. And, according to the story that has been handed down, from generation to generation, it should be so. All one may obtain now is conjecture mingled with tattered recollections that link together those battered vaults and tombstones.

On one, the only one left standing, is recounted the demise of Thomas Biddle West, son of George and Amy West, on May 17, 1826, "after 50 hours illness." That added information has a strange sound to it, as if the boy— he was but fourteen—had perished suddenly and inexplicably. However, it was not until three years later that the Dark Angel took more startling toll.

The next youngest son, James, who was nineteen, died first, on August 24, 1829. Then George, Jr., twenty-three, was stricken down Sept. 3. George, Sr., who was fifty-five, expired Sept. 10. Last of all came the death of the mother, Amy, fifty-two, on Sept. 15. These particulars are plainly inscribed on the broken slabs in a graveyard which, it is said, has been bereft of many of its smaller markers.

They could have died natural deaths, you say—after all this time, no one can be certain. It's just as likely, another may argue, that some frightful plague forced its way into the West homestead, striking down four of its five surviving members but a few days apart. But the legend heard through the countryside has something else to offer. However unjustly, the finger of accusation that pointed to the eldest son, who seems to have been about thirty, does not waver even now. He, the heir, packed up the family belongings, closed the farmhouse, took one last look at the graves on the sandy hill, and drove away, to disappear forever.

Mrs. John Stock, over sixty, who lives in a little red farmhouse down the road, claims to be one of the oldest residents of the vicinity. She has made her home near the site of Catawba for thirty-five years or more.

"Yes," she said, "Catawba was quite a city once—or I guess 'town' would be better. And that story of the supposed murders has been coming down through all the years. There was a Mrs. Joslin in Mays Landing, who died recently at the age of one hundred. She used to say that she was alive at the time of the killings that wiped out all but one of the Wests.

"The Wests, from what we were always given to understand, made up the principal family of Catawba. Up there where you saw the broken vaults, there were other stones. But they've been stolen by now. There was a chapel in front of the little cemetery, too, but it must have burned down. It was left idle after the Wests died so suddenly. This road you see along here was only a woodland trail in those days—it wasn't much more when I came here.

"No," said Mrs. Stock, "I don't remember that I've ever heard the name of the eldest son. He lived in the old house for a short time, they say, and then packed everything up and drove away. Many of the other people in Catawba had been employed on the West farm. One by one they moved off until the town was left a ghostly village with nobody in it."

As time went on, residents of the vicinity wondered about the eldest son who left so mysteriously. Many did more than wonder, making definite accusations concerning the manner in which the others had died. But the heir never once reappeared. After a time there was nothing to show that anything unusual had happened—except those names and dates on the tombstones.

Some fifteen miles from Catawba, beyond Tuckahoe, at Head-of-the-River, is old Etna, another of the furnace towns which once saw much activity. This is one of the

seldom frequented villages of its type and yet, for picturesqueness, its ruin is as interesting as old Weymouth in a
different way. There is nothing to betray its presence down
a dirt road beyond the old church and cemetery. But a
venture through a woodland trail to the bank of the Tuckahoe Creek has a real reward for the explorer.

In the *History and Gazetteer of New Jersey*, loaned the
Lost Town Hunters by the Rev. William H. Stone, of
West Collingswood, the following description appears:

> "ETNA—Furnace and forge, and
> grist and saw mills, on Tuckahoe
> Creek, Weymouth Township, Gloucester
> County, about 15 miles from the sea."

Of the mills there is no trace. But on a point by the river,
now covered by a growth of dense pines and tangled vines,
are sluiceways and canals, meandering between the piles of
leaf-blanketed slag, and mould blackened by charcoal deposits. From the midst of these rises the old furnace chimney, sixty feet high, still possessing a certain majesty. It is
of Jersey stone and brick construction, the bricks retaining
an unusually vivid red hue. There are six obvious thick-
nesses of brick, covered by the layers of stone, accounting
for its remarkable preservation.

Along the shore are the remains of wharves. On the
creek bottom are bits of slag. But the tall carmine chimney,
like the tombstones at Catawba, stands as a gallant sentinel
of days and activities beyond recall.

XXIX

SLABTOWN AND COPANY

EVERY now and then, after we have swallowed great lumps
of history like bad-tasting pills, comes a word, a statement
or a casual revelation that casts the wavering shadow of
doubt on the things we have gone on believing, however
blindly.

In such a light comes the plausible story of Jacksonville,
once Slabtown, of Copany Meeting and Petticoat Bridge,
stealing some of the thunder from that rather easy victory
achieved by Washington at Trenton.

Slabtown, like dozens of other old towns in Burlington
County, will not be found upon a map. Nor will the name
of Copany be discovered a half mile further down the road
from where, in the Jacksonville of today, roads to Smithville, Hedding, Columbus, Mt. Holly, Burlington, and
Jobstown meet. Just the same, both villages have provided
their unsung share in the history of Revolutionary days.

It was in 1863 that Slabtown officially became Jacksonville, and although seventy-three years have spun their webs
on doors and windows of the older houses, some occupants
still show preference for the old name. In its yesteryear
Slabtown boasted two taverns, a mill, fire house, Post Office, and general store. Once it proudly numbered among
its prominent citizens seven fiddlers, three blacksmiths,
three wheelwrights, five storekeepers, two hotelmen and
two preachers. Nowadays, skirted by modern highways

and for the most part, by the traffic that follows them, nearly all is legend and recollection.

Slabtown became Jacksonville upon the petition of its first postmaster. Its original name made it different from others on the fringe of the pine belt and advertised it as a shipping center of slabs, mined in the hills near-by.

Joel King, named Mayor King by the common consent of those who have to do with such things, was born in 1852, and has always lived in Slabtown. He remembers stirring scenes in days of the Civil War, the anxiety of youngsters to get to the front, the periodic visits of recruiting officers to the store by the crossroads. Joel has a countryside reputation for a knowledge of distributing farm fertilizer.

For fifty years Joel has lived in a building that was the school he attended as a boy. Of an evening he looks from the doorway through which he once passed most reluctantly. At night he dreams of the rod, the pigtailed girls and the dyspeptic, metallic-voiced schoolmaster.

Mayor King recalls more vividly one teacher, John R. Howell, who later became a prominent citizen of Mt. Holly. Howell taught at the Slabtown school for a dollar and a half a day, putting up with the pranks and practices of a small room filled with from sixty to seventy-five pupils. Students of the school, he recalls, had to bring two cents for their day's schooling or they just didn't get taught.

Jacksonville is also the home of Ella Mason, who has gained the reputation of being a soothsayer among her Burlington County friends. Ella, once a schoolmate of Warner Hargrove, lives the life of a recluse in the old town. She will not admit that she has "gypsy powers" or that she tells fortunes. She merely says that she reads the cards and they tell her things seldom revealed to other people. She'll read them by daytime, moreover, and never at night.

Ella's father, Uriah Bowker, was a veteran of the Civil War. Following his part in the rebellion he returned home blind. Undaunted, however, he obtained the job of carrying mail from Brown's Mills. His salary was ninety dollars a year.

Uriah depended on the kindness of children and the services of a little yellow mutt dog to guide him to the addresses scrawled on his letters. With these aides there was little difficulty in covering the road between the Mills and the railroad station at New Lisbon. Bowker was a jolly fellow in spite of his affliction, and is remembered plodding along the roadway, surrounded by a throng of laughing children and the happy, dancing little dog.

For years and years Uriah went on with his work, supporting thereby his wife and three small children. Then Martin Hargrove, a pension attorney for the Department of the Interior at Washington, secured for the faithful postman payment of one hundred dollars a month, dating back to the year he went blind. Uriah obtained quite a fortune in one lump sum.

The first disposition of the money was made at the suggestion of the eldest son, Harvey, who declared a dollar should be expended for a new axe. This was sympathy of a kind for Mrs. Bowker who for years, almost exclusively, had cut the wood for the family bin.

Perhaps one of the most characteristic dwellings of Jacksonville is what was once the Post Office and general store. It is a frame building, shingled, with a strange triangular shape. Doors and windows are closed now, some of them are barred against inquisitive intruders. In the mustiness that goes with ancient houses, long shut up, lives a kindly old lady who once had the proud distinction of being Jacksonville's postmistress.

Smiling and quaint, she is Miss Jane Isabell Rogers, if you please. It was Miss Rogers' father who built the house in which she lives, and for years he was postmaster, too. Miss Rogers, in a way, fell heir to the post and kept it for eighteen years. Later, with the installation of the free delivery system, business simmered to nothing. Miss Rogers told us she merely shut up shop and called it a day.

For all its uncertain appearance outside, the house tells its story unaided, with its doors and paneling of solid oak, door-knobs, hinges and locks of solid brass, all fashioned in the serviceable style of the days that produced them. But Miss Rogers discounted all these things to talk of the electric fixtures she installed only a few years ago. It has been a comparatively short time, you see, that Jacksonville has known electric light. "But," Miss Rogers declared, "even the streets will have them here one of these days."

Slabtown was originally on the main coach and mail road and its hostelries often echoed with the small talk of travelers and the shuffle of rustic dances.

"I remember it all as if it were only yesterday," Miss Rogers smiled, shaking her head a little sadly. "We had two public houses here, you see. Life was a gay whirl then with the visitors filling the hotel and men of business stopping overnight. There were plenty of parties, informal affairs, you know, and then, every once in so often a REAL affair at the tavern. Music . . . dancing . . . pretty girls . . . handsome young men . . . all that went with merry evenings. You'd never dream all that happened here, looking at the old town now, would you?" Miss Rogers roused suddenly from her memories.

The hotel is more than one hundred years old and has had a checkered career. Once you could get a stiff beaker there for three cents—and now? Why, even the roads and fields are parched like desert sands.

Close by, living in a stately old house, built in 1721, is a distinguished resident, whom we dare not call old. Comparison with the broken roads and ancient houses of Slabtown makes all its people seem quite young. This fellow said his name was Styer. For him, too, those tavern days are just behind, somewhere out of sight and around the corner. Barn dances at near-by farms, gay days and freer nights are memories that made his twinkling eyes dance with new light.

Mr. Styer said that Slabtown was a favorite haunt of the "Jersey Devil" in the old days. That uncertain monster, for many years making mysterious returns to widely separated sections of South Jersey, took particular delight in staging sensational appearances on dark, misty roads after Slabtown dances were over, waving his wings, hissing green fire and lashing his scaly tail. Time and time again fair dancers would run squealing to porticos, escorts would be suddenly bowled over in bramble-lined ditches and couples would cling together as frightened horses sent buggies reeling along rutted roads.

Mr. Styer said that it was only twenty-five years ago that the present little church was built. After that a modern school was put up. The quaint, brightly painted house of worship, on whose lawn peach festivals are still occasions of great moment, is the scene of services only every second Sunday. It is the Jacksonville Presbyterian Church. Its pastor divides his labors between Jacksonville and another church at Hedding.

Slabtown was a business center once. Mr. Styer told us, "Yes, indeed, we even had a grist and sawmill. The Mill was Rigg's Mill. Ed Rigg, you don't remember him? Well, he was an uncle of Charley Rigg, you know, the former judge over to Mt. Holly."

Slabtown built up for itself a subtle reputation for being a village where people vanished without trace. Pressing for data along these lines for details, however, availed us little. Only one name could be given us, that of Elmer Shinn, a wealthy stock farmer, whose strongly built and dignified brick house, after the fashion of the 60s, still stands near-by. Twenty years or so ago Elmer dropped from sight and from that day to this, the story goes, has neither been seen nor heard from.

One old building, a shingle-covered frame, was the headquarters of a local fraternal order, but no one in town could definitely tell us just what group it was. On the "façade" could be distinguished the inscription, "Enterprise Council," but the actual name of the lodge has been erased by time and weather. Pigeons roost on the signboard now.

Slabtown's introduction to the automobile age was all but marked by tragedy. Early models of the "horseless buggy" seldom sought out places of Slabtown's size and as a result it was many years before such towns saw any. Wagon roads were not especially conducive to the first solid tires.

However, there came a day when a new driver, a prominent Burlington woman, selected the Jacksonville road to practise driving. It was her second time abroad. She knew two essentials about her shiny new machine: How to start and how to steer it. Everything went well until Jacksonville was reached. There the driver, goggled and scarfed and dustered, beheld with alarm a country mother, with her brood of eight, stretched out across the dusty highway.

The driver honked the horn, then she pulled at the bell, which was supposed to be an emergency warning. The reaction was opposite from the one desired. The little family, never having seen this modern miracle before, stood its ground, fear paralyzing limbs and masking faces, as the noisy contraption approached. Unable to stop because she had forgotten how, the woman on the high seat wove in and out among the pedestrian group at the terrifying speed of fifteen miles an hour.

The appearance and disappearance of the new invention left Jacksonville in a daze for a long time, with merchants and old-fashioned householders warning children of the invading "red devils." Such narratives lurk beneath the sagging porches, the crumbling foundations and tarnished memories of another town that will not admit itself forgotten.

Down the road is Copany. All it owns is a deserted Friends' Meeting house, an adjacent farm and a bridge that succeeds a span that once made the hamlet famous.

Did it ever strike you, while reading the colorful and over-zealously detailed descriptions of the Battle at Trenton, that there might have been something else besides Yuletide cheer and tipsiness behind that rather easy win? Respectfully viewing the situation, reluctantly casting even a momentary doubt, did it ever seem to you that the Hessians were rather willing, as well as bewildered captives?

U. S. Grant Troxell, of No. 1 Warren Street, Beverly,

has a strange but exceedingly plausible story to tell regarding that battle, preceded by a prelude with locale at Copany. Here on a brow of a hill is the square meeting house with its date, 1775, plainly contrasted in darker brick. Behind it is a small burial plot, protected by a broken iron fence in addition to a formidable-looking bull, grazing the day we ventured there.

Here it was, according to Mr. Troxell, that the Hessians first learned against whom they were to fight. It is a family story, handed down, father to son. Mr. Troxell's grandfather was General John Christian Troxell, in command of the Hessians, who, marching along the Slabtown-Copany road, were on their way to Trenton.

It is Mr. Troxell's contention that the Hessians were hired by the British to come over and help them fight, and that they were never officially informed who their adversaries were to be. At Copany they found out for the first time, he says, that they were fighting the Yankees. In those days one could plausibly expect to fight Indians, wild men of the jungle or most anything.

It was in 1777 that the Hessians, leaving the King's Highway, cut across country. The women of Slabtown and vicinity, duly informed of the approaching soldiers, highly incensed by the advance of foemen who were hired foreigners, raced down and began frantically ripping up planks of the bridge. The stream at that time was much deeper than you'll find it today.

These women patriots who have never been justly commemorated, so far as we know, were led by a woman whose anxiety to serve the Yankee cause all but cost her life. As she removed the final plank, she slipped, and if her petticoat hadn't caught on a nail, holding her secure until rescued, she would have tumbled, head first, in the deep surge of the creek. From that day to this the natives of the country-side refer to the span as the "petticoat bridge."

It was perhaps the sight of the women that gave the Hessians their first knowledge of their enemy. The Americans had left a small force behind and this company established itself in the Copany meeting house, from the windows and makeshift apertures of which they opened fire on the files of advancing troops, bent on fording near the damaged bridge.

Another legend is that the meeting house was used merely as a temporary Revolutionary hospital. This version is chosen by many persons who disbelieve the story of the bloody hand-marks on the white walls of the loft and the decidedly gruesome stains on the woodwork. At first we were among the scoffers, although Mr. Troxell declared soberly that the marks were there and that the matter was no fabrication at all.

The stains, which many believe to be in the gallery, are in the cramped loft above it, from where the brave defenders, bleeding from their wounds, are supposed to have kept up a feeble defense of the road.

How the tide of battle went at Copany is not definitely recorded. The Hessians, crippled somewhat by snipers' fire, moved on to Columbus and Rising Sun Square, near Bordentown. After reaching Trenton the force was split, half going to Monmouth. At Columbus they camped around the houses now occupied by Mrs. Alice Walters and Howard Archer, which served as a hasty headquarters.

Mr. Troxell declares that the Hessians, having surrendered at Trenton, moved on to central Pennsylvania where they were given plots to cultivate. Troxell's grandfather, the Hessian General, at one time owned all the land which is now Easton. The property, granted by Washington, was sold bit by bit until Troxell owned very little himself.

The Copany meeting house is surely one of the best preserved in this section. On its first floor are the rows of unpainted, straight-backed benches, in a small square room with walls half panelled in walnut. On the floor is matting and old rag-carpet. The silken cushions on the benches are frayed and moth-eaten.

The second floor is a sort of overflow gallery, with doors that can be lowered as a ceiling. Here are tiers of backless benches, with initials carved in them, attained by exceedingly winding but solid stairs—two sets of them.

There is also the usual adjustable partition which separated the men and women attending meeting. Old booklets of minutes, tracing the activities of various meetings to two States, lie on the benches. The place has not been used since 1904.

Beside the structure is a farmhouse, which in 1900 was the scene of a suspected poisoning, a County constable being the supposed victim. His wife was indicted, it is recalled, but later was completely exonerated by a jury.

So, surrounded by such spirited glories of old, Copany is forgotten. With undecorated Revolutionary soldiers' graves in its burial plot, the sniping holes of its walls now filled in, the meeting house rarely achieves the attention from the passer-by. Such details of history cannot be plucked from the air. Lowing cattle graze in the meadow near "Petticoat Bridge." Motorized carryalls and tractors bump along the dusty road.

In the worn books upon its benches there are many names prominent in the locality, Howells, Stokeses, Atkinsons, Asays and Harrises. There are also the names of forgotten towns, Martha Furnace, Harrisia, Mary Ann Forge. Now Copany and Jacksonville find themselves rolling downhill toward the same forgetfulness.

In the loft of the Copany Friends' Meeting old residents point to the bloody hand-marks of Continental soldiers who tried to prevent a company of Hessians from reaching Trenton in 1777.

Mount Misery, once a prosperous stage stopover and a center of the charcoal industry. The hotel and a few decaying houses survived well into the twentieth century.

XXX

FORSAKEN MOUNT MISERY

THIS is the story of Mount Misery, the town that has forgotten why it was given such a miserable name.

On a winding, narrow, brush-grown trail through the deer woods, east of what was Ong's Hat and south of what used to be Hanover Furnace, is a lone dwelling. For exactly two hundred years, according to the stories they tell, it has stood here, defying the ravages of time and the weather of long years. So it has watched in wondering silence the huts about it tumble to decay.

This was the Mount Misery Hotel. Inside you can see a mouldy old closet where powerful liquors were stored. And too, there is a small aperture in the wall of a high-ceiling tap-room, through which were passed the cups that cheered. These were days before the bar of later times was introduced, days before Aunt Sallie and "Cad," their box telephone and Mount Misery's Town Car.

Peter Bard was first owner of the land on which Mount Misery was later founded. Peter was an early emigrant from Montpelier in France, the son of Bennet Bard, one of the early Huguenots.

Bard came to America to escape the religious persecution of the homeland, bringing his wife, Dinah, and their two small children to the Province of West New Jersey.

Peter has been written down, in tradition at least, as a man of great industry, intelligence and philanthropy. Shortly after his arrival he established himself at Burlington as a merchant, and continued in the business until 1723.

Meanwhile he had been appointed by Robert Hundter, then Governor of New Jersey, as one of the judges and justices of the peace in the County of Burlington, an office of much responsibility in those days. He held this position of esteem from 1717 until 1721. Although the job undoubtedly paid something, there is no record that he took any action in lawsuits until the last year.

Peter was primarily a real estate man, and certainly one of the first realty dealers on record in New Jersey. He started buying and selling property as a side line in 1715 and there are a number of deeds which trace his activities at the time. These transfers include many acres of timber, saw-mill sites and iron works.

One of the early deeds definitely shows that he acquired what was then called Mount Misery Mill. He sold some of the property after a short time, in 1723, to John Monroe and his wife. There is a queer wording in the document which shows that two "half parts" went also to John West and John Bispham. The Monroes later transferred their property to the Hanover Farms tract in which it still remains.

Peter Bard retained ownership of sixty-six acres at Mount Misery Mill which, for purposes of identification, was called Peter Bard's Cedar Mill. Peter called the property in general, Montpelier Lands, in honor of his birthplace. In 1723 he gave up his Burlington shop and went to live in the tract. Of how the name Mount Misery came into existence there is no record. It is supposed that a near-by stream of water bore the title, bestowed perhaps by Indians.

The location is on a slight elevation but there is nothing

that resembles a mountain. The climb is scarcely notice-able because of the dense woods.

One of the most authentic stories connected with the vil-lage is that in later years one George B. Upton, of Boston, took over the property after making a loan of $90,000 for its improvements. Then he came to inspect it. Perhaps the view of this vast twenty-five thousand acres presented a desolate, miserable sight.

But Upton was determined on making a real town of it. He started in motion the clearing of timber in the vicinity which continued on through the Civil War and until less than thirty-five years ago. This timber was cut by various companies and individuals for market and "coal wood." Making charcoal was an industry in the surrounding coun-try and Mount Misery became its unofficial headquarters.

Though an army of optimistic and earnest workers had preceded him, it was a native "Piney," Charles Pittman, who was perhaps most prominently identified as a leader of activities in Mount Misery. Pittman, despite his lack of education, made himself a kind of super-foreman, and had carte blanche with the owner. Supplied with the money of Upton and his heirs, Pittman built from a so-so hamlet that had dawdled through more than a century a village of con-siderable importance and population.

There were nearly one hundred homes, a village school that served for day sessions on weekdays and religious de-votions on Sunday, a village store and a hotel. This hotel is one of the few buildings standing in Mount Misery. Here Pittman lived to a ripe old age, to see the town he hoped would disprove its name go on with expectations. When he died, however, most of these aspirations died with him.

Here in this gaunt building that once echoed with the cries of wassail and loud talk of the transient, lived "Aunt Sallie" Pittman, the widow of Mount Misery's promoter, wood-chopper, teamster and charcoal-burner. Here in Mount Misery, miles from a Post Office, from railroads and banks and real towns, Charley was esteemed and chosen for many posts of importance in Jersey's backwoods.

When we rediscovered Mount Misery, Aunt Sallie lived there with her daughter, Miss Caroline. They were the town's only inhabitants, with the exception of Levi Eckman, the "man-about." Levi found plenty to do, for the women kept a little farm and raised poultry.

"Cad," as they called Caroline, could tell her visitors of the many snakes—big rattlers, too—that she killed. Only that summer she got one, she said, but not before it had killed the mother of a brood of young turkeys. One of Cad's stories was of the time when she went deep into the woods with her father and saw a surprised mother snake swallow eighteen young rattlers in order to protect them from possible harm.

Gardening isn't easy at Mount Misery. The deer, Cad told us, would eat the garden products as fast as they grew. Fences wouldn't deter them: full-grown deer leap over six-foot barriers with the utmost ease.

Of the town's forgotten residents there are many memories. Benjamin Dunbarr was the town cooper and in the vicinity they still produce a stout cedar bucket or tub and say, "This was made by 'Ben Dunn.'" Ben was a naturalist and his talks were more than entertaining to those who visited Mount Misery in palmy days. Ben was a fiddler, too, providing spirited music for many gay parties. He had several wives—perhaps he married some of them—but he couldn't get along well with women and consequently lived recurrently by himself. In later years, he painted a warning on the door of his hovel to stave off unwanted callers.

Abel Harker and his son, John Henry, operated Mount Misery's sawmill. John Henry once told Warner Hargrove, of Pemberton, how as a boy he had thrillingly celebrated the Fourth of July. Given a holiday and five cents he started off for a gorgeous day. After using three pennies to buy old-time "hossie cakes" for his dinner, he walked to Brown's Mills and back, a distance of twelve miles, to mark the big occasion, keeping that precious two cents change.

There was "English Charlie" Hicks, too, Bill Hibbins, "Dutch" Ernest Cline, Bob Harris, Jerry Hults, "Scotch Alex" Ross, Mahlon Joslin, "Wes" and Zare Foulks and their spinster sisters, Liza and Clarissa. And among old residents of Mount Misery whom Aunt Sallie recalled, were Mike and Tom Bowker. But the woods have swallowed them up. Only Hicks and Harris are in the vicinity, living the simple life and telling stories that should have made Trader Horn sail to the Arctic.

Here, apart from most things, was a simple people, who lived humbly, loved honestly, sent children off to school, laughed across their rude tables and thanked God for happiness. Now there is only Cad to remember and tell about them. Aunt Sallie died two summers ago.

Cad didn't say how long she'd stay but it wasn't in her mind, apparently, to leave the home town. She has a telephone that's been kept working for years—"since the contraption was first installed." She gets her mail from a rural route several miles away.

The Pittman home is still a hotel in one sense, for here, back from the roads of modern days, unknown to the ac-

coutrements of present-day households, there lingers a
friendly hospitality. Aunt Sallie and Cad used to prepare
meals for their passing friends; meals worth talking about,
which included many strange but tasty dishes. But through
their utter lack of interest in what the rest of the world was
doing, we could see that they knew that Mount Misery
must soon be forgotten forever, along with the towns that
used to be.

Water wizard Frank Peck and his dog. The cannonball mold
beside him is one he found at Batsto.

XXXI

INDIANS AND THE WIZARD

THE world, to you and me, is a place of banks and magazines and days that click on schedule. We worry over money and fretfully snatch our entertainment from absurdities. Refusing to take things as we find them, we make up all sorts of fables for our own amusement. Then, when we come upon things that are a little strange or inexplicable, we brand them as untrue.

Out in the back-country of the pines, where banks are woolen socks and where mails arrive three times a week, you're compelled to believe in the almost impossible, time and again. There's the story of the Ong's Hat watermelon that served two men a whole month and there's the legend of the town hog-killer who slew several thousand higher than he could count. And then there's the story of Indian Ann and the Water Wizard.

Ann was the last Indian at Indian Mills, New Jersey's last Indian Reservation. Located on the road from Medford to Hammonton through the pinelands, it is not quite forgotten, but rather, a town that forgot to grow up.

A plan made of the village of Indian Mills in 1876 shows that there were fourteen buildings standing and in operation. One was a church, another a sawmill, two were stores and ten were tiny homes. Today's Indian Mills is some distance removed from that of long ago. Most of the old buildings are gone and only a rusted wheel shows where

the mill once stood. The second mill has vanished altogether.

The old village is remembered as the first speculative real
estate development in South Jersey. In the interval between 1850 or 1856, Indian Mills was advertised as a "paper
town" and hopes were voiced that it would in a short time
become a thriving city. A flattering prospectus was issued.
Residents who wanted to realize a lot of money quickly
were invited to make Indian Mills their home. The hand-
bills didn't call it Indian Mills. In the large-lettered notices
it was Fruitland.

The city with the fruity name never came into being.
Instead, the town was known for a long while as Edgepol-
lock. The Indians who lived there on land given them by
the Government were called "Edgepollocks." In their day
a missionary, John Brainerd, lived in town, in a small dwelling not far from the humming sawmill. John passed on
as did the last of the Indians, but his house, now owned by
Geoffrey Hancock, can still be pointed out.

In those days the Indians themselves operated the sawmill. It was one of the few mills anywhere in the country
owned and operated by Redskins. Near-by was a little
church in which the Indians conducted their own services.
Behind it was a burying-ground reserved for those who
died expecting the glories of the Happy Hunting Ground.

These were times prior to the attempted realty boom.
By 1825, the last of the tribe, about one hundred in number, had moved to a reservation in New York State, leaving
behind a single family of half-breeds.

The church in which the Indians had worshipped was
later used by the whites for divine services until, in 1802, it
burned down. On the site was erected a one-room school,

which many of the older residents of the Indian Mills of today recall attending. The school has no classes any more and in season is used for cranberry sorting. Pupils now go by bus to a central school.

We found no evidence at all of the Indian burying-ground, back of the school. Here under the waving Indian grass, in ground that has yielded its corn and sweet potatoes, sleep South Jersey's last Red Men. It is amusing to discover down this selfsame road, that one of the biggest buildings in the surrounding country is the Red Men's Hall.

Mahlon Prickett, Indian Mills' oldest resident, who attended the old "Indian school," vividly recalled to us the days when the graves of the cemetery could be easily found. Prickett, John Miller and James M. Armstrong, other citizens, well remember Indian Ann. There is some discrepancy about her name. On the plains and in the pines further north they call her Ann. Here in Indian Mills, her erstwhile home, she is Kate. Ann or Kate, she was a colorful character.

Indian Ann, who died about 1890, the last of a tribe that had long deserted her, had three husbands, and she outlived all of them.

Number one was John Roberts, a colored man; number two, Pat Burke, an Irishman; and number three, Lewis Marhoff, a high-yellow. Marhoff, they say, was a more than remarkable fellow. He was over seven feet tall and had hands like hams, knotted with muscles, and capable of crushing anything in their viselike grip.

Ann's life is another of the legends of the lost towns. Of her connection with the Edgepollocks little is known. She is said to have been the mother of five children, all of whom preceded her to their reward. She often visited the sur-

rounding towns, selling trinkets and woven baskets, boldly
intruding in a world that found her out of place.

When Ann came to town, people used to point and say,
"Look, there's Indian Ann!" And then they'd tell some
story about her or one of her husbands. Nowadays, many
people from Browns Mills, Medford, and Mt. Holly,
proudly declare reminiscently, "Sure, I remember her."

The name of Aaron Burr, a Justice of the Peace, detective and lawyer of old Burlington County, has a connection
in Indian Mills. Years ago, they told us, he used to dig for
relics in the old Indian cemetery. Once he unearthed a shin
bone that measured thirty inches, attesting the giant proportions of some of those last Indians. On another occasion
Aaron was officially censured for rooting about in the
graveyard. There was something of a rumpus once when
an opposing attorney referred to him as a "ghoul" in Mt.
Holly court.

Armstrong, whose little farm is outside Indian Mills,
down the old Atsion road and not the main highway, has in
his possession an undated map which shows how lots were
cut after the reservation was abandoned. At that time the
land was bought by various individuals. The offers were
extremely attractive then, for Governmental red tape, pro-
verbially slow, had not yet provided for the collection of
taxes. Many who bought land on the former Indian haven
lived there some time before paying any levies at all.

The case reached the Supreme Court before decision was
found. It finally was concluded in 1885 and since then
householders have been paying taxes, like residenters elsewhere.

Those who remember Ann say that her age, far beyond

the century mark, was due to a determination to live until she could sleep in a wigwam.

One of her "children," the story goes, finally built her one. Pleased and relieved and chattering to herself, she tossed a blanket about her and went into the teepee. Somebody who looked in a while later saw that she seemed to be asleep.

It was the sleep from which there is no awakening. Indian Ann was dead.

We had been looking for the Water Wizard for several weeks. Finally, we heard that he had lived near Indian Mills, on the Tabernacle-Red Lion Road. But Charles Remine, of Wrightstown, told us we were misinformed, that while he did live on that road, his home was in Red Lion—that is, if you could put him in any town. So we found him.

For years Frank Peck has been spoken of as "the Water Wizard." Pineys, who never read or wrote a line and never found out his Christian name, have talked about him as one of their own miracle men. He is the man, who, walking in a field with a bit of forked stick in his hand, can tell the well-drillers where to hunt for water. Never once has he been wrong!

In the countryside, water is ordinarily obtained from a spring, a creek or a pond. If there are none of these, a well must be dug. First of all, however, much labor and time are saved if it is definitely known where there is a subterranean stream. This is Frank Peck's business. Water hunters, instead of drilling three or four worthless test wells as they would perhaps have to do, call on him for help.

Frank was seventy-seven, when we saw him. If it weren't for that rheumatic limp, you'd put his age at ten years less than that. His figure was gaunt and his face lean. He had a full, unkempt grayish beard. His eyes were keen, and a bluish-gray. Frank had a way of looking right through you, reproaching any disbelief in his powers that you might be trying to hide.

Here on the road he lived in a tiny but comfortable house, a small unpainted dwelling, with his wife. His sons had moved away. Other relatives, here and there, proudly boasted their kinship, and believed implicitly in his mysterious gifts in finding water. Frank said he was but one of three persons who could do it, and he wouldn't tell us who the others were.

We found the Water Wizard at his back door. His shirt was open at the front, but he didn't seem to mind the chill wind that presaged the northeaster. He had recently been ill at the Burlington County hospital, but he didn't care to talk about that.

"They told us you were the Water Wizard," we began, "and we were wondering if you'd tell us about it."

Frank Peck smiled and started at once to look for a stick. Unsheathing his pocket knife, he said his divining rod must be forked and green, with a six-inch "handle" and prongs about eighteen inches long. These prongs, he declared, must be about the size of one's little finger.

Grasping such a forked stick by the prongs, Uncle Frank started walking slowly over his land. The first stick broke and he had to hunt another, cut from a young peach tree. Then he began to walk again, maintaining an impressive silence. His face took on an unearthly stare. His eyes fixed on space. The cold breeze played in his straggly gray hair.

Then, with the "handle" pointing away from him, the prongs began to twist despite his grip. The "handle" slowly turned toward the ground.

"There's water!" Frank said, and loosened his hold. He exhaled sharply.

Beginning some distance from the already indicated underground stream, the Water Wizard approached again. This time we watched his taut white hands, skeptically perhaps. When he came to the water, the stick went down again and we saw that there was no hokum about it. Uncle Frank's grip was one of steel. When he opened his palms there were bits of bark in them.

"How do you do it? What is this mysterious power?" we asked.

The Wizard smiled. "I can't explain it," he said.

"Where did you learn about it? Did your father do it?"

"No, no," he laughed. "I was past middle age when I started. Not everyone can do it, you see. I've tried other people, but it won't work, somehow."

That the modern world is not all scoff and skepticism is shown in the business Frank gets. He's much in demand in Medford Lakes, where cottagers have been sinking wells. Other developers are glad to pay Frank five dollars for sure knowledge of where water is, knowledge that saves them a hundred or more.

Years ago, Frank said he saw someone, some other wizard, in action, and he's been at it ever since.

Uncle Frank revealed himself as a smithy, too. His equipment was mostly out-of-doors. Despite his age, he was busy, he said. "Water-finding's a good business," he told us, "but it's not regular. There aren't many blacksmiths nowadays, and that evens it up."

In Colonial times a manor house with a picturesque little summer house overlooked the lake at Hanover Furnace. Now the site is part of Fort Dix. Below, the late M. Warner Hargrove and the slag heap that used to mark the site of the Furnace.

XXXII

HANOVER FURNACE

SOME time ago, while excavations were being made near Valley Forge, Pennsylvania, iron cannonballs were unearthed bearing the stamp of Hanover Furnace. Hanover Furnace, if you will refer to your map of Southern New Jersey, is apparently the name of a tiny hamlet, several miles northwest of Brown's Mills. Actually, there is no Hanover Furnace.

A bustling town of at least a thousand population, and two hundred homes in Revolutionary days, Hanover Furnace is today but a series of clearings in which a brick can be kicked up here and there in the undergrowth.

The date of actual founding of the town is unknown but Hanover must have been in full operation during the Colonial war days. The earliest picture known to be in existence is a daguerreotype, dated 1856, which was owned by Warner Hargrove, of Pemberton.

This picture shows what was then called The Mansion House, a well-constructed Colonial dwelling of possibly twenty rooms, standing on a promontory overlooking a lake and surrounded by trees that could not have been native to the pine belt. The garden that grew in front of the house is plainly seen, with a little summer house at the water's edge.

On the site today there is no evidence of the house. The trees have gone and a few of their saplings sway in their place. In among the tall, brown Indian grass, however, are

cultivated strawberry plants, rose bushes and a few unkempt greens that show where the garden was. The picture indicates the village in the background, but all of this—
church, schoolhouse, and the rest—has gone.

Before iron was discovered in the mountains of Pennsylvania, the only known source for obtaining pig iron for
commercial purposes was in the New Jersey bogs of the
pine area. From this a cheap ore was taken, its appearance
resembling coke except for its chocolate color. This ore
was first dug out, and then hauled by wheelbarrow, mule
or ox-team to the furnace.

The location of the furnace at Hanover is shown today
by a huge heap of discard, among which can be found pans
and pokers and other Jersey-made articles. The slag is
being redug for use in improving near-by roads.

When the supply of this ore became exhausted, residents
of Hanover Furnace held on for a time and then, family by
family, sought more prosperous places.

Few persons remain who can tell the stories they heard
of Hanover's heyday and the people who lived in its boom
days. Furnace workers were employed not only in digging
the ore and operating the furnace but in cutting down
many acres of virgin pine for conversion into charcoal. It is
only within the last hundred years that anthracite coal has
displaced charcoal as a chief means of fuel.

Charcoal was carted to market by hundreds of teams
drawing what were then known as "charcoal boxes," from
Hanover Furnace. These vehicles had the appearance of inverted cones. They were about sixteen feet long and carried, at capacity, one hundred bushels of charcoal. Evidence of Hanover's trade can still be plainly seen where the
topsoil has broken away to reveal the inky subsurface.

Charcoal was made by cutting timber into convenient lengths and piling it in cone shape, first to a height of about ten feet. This cone was covered with turf taken from the woods and again covered with sand to make the pile airtight, except for the draft at the bottom, opening at the top. A slow fire was then maintained for days.

After cooling, the cones were uncovered and rakes with long teeth were used to pull the brands from the fire. These were put into baskets having the appearance of large turtle shells. Thence they went to the "coal-boxes." Although some residents remember charcoal-burning as a premier industry in Burlington County, all but one or two of the burners have long since departed, as finally as Hanover Furnace.

There was once a factory at Hanover Furnace, they say, making nail kegs and iron nails of varying lengths.

During the Revolution, it became necessary to erect cannon for the defense of Marcus Hook. Hanover Furnace moulded a cannon of huge proportions, mounted it on a specially constructed wagon and sent it away, drawn by an eight-ox team to be one of South Jersey's mammoth contributions to the nation's defense.

But, the story goes, the cannon never arrived. The wagon was mired near Pemberton and the cannon went overboard into a creek, where, according to tradition, it still is. They have always called the stream Cannon Run.

Many smaller cannon were made at Hanover. It was the custom to prove them, by shooting a ball straight into the woods. An occasional ball is brought to light, even in these late days, by berry-pickers. Hargrove had one, a twenty-five pounder, in his Pemberton office.

Only a few years ago you could stroll along Delaware

Avenue in Philadelphia and find cannon inverted in the ground as curb line buttresses. Several of these bore the Hanover Furnace stamp.

Thousands of acres in the vicinity of Hanover were formerly owned by the Jones Estate. About 1860, two brothers, who had fallen heir, decided to divide. At Brown's Mills, on the north shore of what is called Mirror Lake, a large stone was put in and it is still looked upon as the division line. North of this line, the section that includes Hanover was owned by Richard Jones.

Some old-timers told us that Jones became deeply involved financially and made a loan of $15,000, giving a blanket mortgage and 1000 acres of the pine-covered property in return. Jones lost his holdings and the ownership came to a mysterious Frederick Pepper. If there is a man of this name and he is the owner, he has never seen Hanover Furnace, the Pineys swear, although the taxes have been paid for more than fifty years without a break.

Over thirty years ago the dam at the end of the lake was carried away by a freshet. An orchard, marshes where water is browned by residue of ore deposits, a row of elms that undoubtedly once lined Main Street, are all that remain of Hanover Furnace.

Hannah Foulks, who operates a road stand near Pemberton, was Hanover Furnace's last known resident. Hannah was evicted from her home during the World War when bullets soared over Hanover from the Camp Dix training grounds. Hannah remembered the stories of the Furnace and the tumble-down schoolhouse, but of the intervening years between moulding of Revolutionary cannon and whistling bullets of a newer wartime, she knew very little.

XXXIII

RED LION

You have heard the story of Caddie Pittman who had to kill rattlesnakes around her home at Mount Misery so they wouldn't kill the chickens. What is more, you've read of the Civil War veteran of New Egypt who told the world that he had killed 74,250 hogs in his lifetime.

This is the story of Red Lion.

You will find it by referring to a map of New Jersey and tracing the southernmost line of Burlington County. It is northwest of Medford Lakes and southeast of Pemberton. For some reason or other the letters of the town's name are second only to Medford and as large as Four Mile, and even Medford Lakes.

Red Lion has always been known as a "large settlement," but as a matter of fact there are very few houses. When you are in "the center of town" no more than eight houses can be seen.

The most prominent of all the town's buildings is one of three stories, red brick and of considerable size. This, if you please, is the Red Lion Hotel, a hostelry which, they say, could tell a story all its own. The hotel took its name from the town and the town got its name—well, here's one story we heard:

The original settlers were people by the name of Parks. No one seems to know from where they came nor exactly when. It was long before the present inhabitants can remember, but the story of how the town was named has been handed down from the Parks, father to son, for several generations.

About half a mile from the settlement is what is known as the Bear Swamp. Bear were plentiful once through this locality and were hunted, in season and out of season, by earlier inhabitants. This town, before it had any definite name, was supposed to be a base for such hunters. They used the settlement at the crossroads as a sort of headquarters for their expeditions.

Here at the intersection of the winding trails that lead to Tabernacle, Beaverville, Vincentown, Friendship and Medford, the hunters gathered in those long-ago days, to take vengeance on the wild animals that were nightly attacking their cattle. But on this occasion the huntsmen failed to find even a bear. However, after the "posse" departed, the same conditions prevailed and Old Man Parks resolved to do a little hunting by himself.

He thought he was going out in search of a bear. Actually he was to meet a lion and get a name for his home town. He came upon it one day, a mountain lion, crouched at the edge of a cedar swamp.

Parks shot at the lion and wounded it. Then his gun failed. He was compelled to grapple with the animal hand-to-hand. He clubbed at its head and it clawed at him. Blood flowed freely. The yellow beast, covered with gore, seemed to turn red, as it expired.

Parks finally brought his kill to town and the town became Red Lion.

Following erection of the hotel in the good old days when a license for selling strong liquors, fork lightning compared to what the ultra-moderns call laughing soup, could be had for the asking, if one was deemed necessary,

the inn hung out a sign with the picture of a brilliant carmine lion above its name, "The Red Lion Hotel."

Since the coming and passing of Prohibition, the hotel
has figured now and then in the news as the enforcement
forces conducted their business. But despite the number
of times the place has spattered the court records at Mount
Holly under different managements, the hotel appears a
peaceful place, a building that remembers a town of other
days and times, that were, undoubtedly, much merrier.

On the opposite corner there is a building which is also
public, a combination gas station, general store and pool-
room. Our visit here was as to some great institution of
which there are fewer each year. The day was cold, skies
were dismal and inside, around the stove, was most of the
town's male population.

It was here that we learned the story of how Red Lion
was named. It is here that many such stories were told,
some of them flavored with peanut shells, sticky candy, fiz-
zing pop and the click of billiard balls. Here wars are won
and family troubles are ironed out in the advice of a powerful congress, offered free.

The best times for planting are decided at the Antrim
Store. Religion is pounded and expounded and sometimes
cast aside. Old times are praised and exiled. Prophecies are
made and dreams built in the haze of tobacco smoke. Marriage, hard times, great statesmen, and disarmament are dis-
cussed with authority and confounding foresight. Of
course, everything from candles to oil and rope and edibles
is sold but these provide only casual interruptions to the
sober senate in session.

Red Lion may be a greater town some day. A concrete
cross-State highway has been constructed cutting close to

this strange-named village. With autos swinging through on the new route to the seashore, there is no limit to its future, especially with a story like Red Lion's.

The general store at the crossroads hamlet of Red Lion. The rambling old Red Lion Hotel is said to have been built in 1710.

XXXIV

THE COUGH THAT NAMED A TOWN: HOCKAMICK

Towns of the pines have been named for hats, chairs, lions, beavers and states of mind. But this one, named for a man with a cough, takes a prize all its own.

Hockamick is a mere cluster of unpainted, weather-beaten houses beside a ruined mill. On the map you'll find it a tiny name south of New Egypt, on a little lake that hangs across the line dividing Burlington and Ocean Counties. The town itself, if it deserves such distinction, appears to be in two counties.

Hockamick—what a strange name! The first explanation we had of it was that one of the Micks, a family prominent in the pines, was a hawker, a traveling salesman hawking miscellaneous goods. Hawker Mick, they told us, was his name. Hawker Mick became Hawking Mick and later, Hockamick. That was the transition of it.

But just as every story of the pinelands is told with variations, this explanation has a more picturesque telling:

This particular Mick was no hawker at all, other informants told us. What identified him was a raucous, disturbing and characteristic cough. In those days before cough drops and on those trails without medicine men, there was no thought of even temporary treatment. Perhaps this was one of those nervous coughs that punctuate the existence of erratic people. At any rate Mick had a cough and everybody knew it.

They used to hear him coming along the road at night. Sometimes you could tell where he was by a lantern he carried. Mostly he toted no light, stepping familiarly along the narrow road, coughing, always coughing.

In the dictionary of the uncouth, to cough is "to hock." To the dwellers thereabouts, Mick "hocked." So the town became Hockamick.

Hockamick it still is but there is little to give it claim for place upon the map. The way to Hockamick leads along a sandy, rutted track that climbs and winds across the fields. Beside the road there is occasionally a house, or more often a hut, where rusted tools, unkempt but tenanted poultry yards and wisps of smoke from the chimneys betray lazy occupancy.

The few remaining residents of the town told us the old mill was established about 1770 or 1780. It was in continuous operation, they said, providing all sorts of lumber for the pine towns. It was said to have been longest in continuous operation in the County and the last lumber mill in the area operated by water power. Now the Hockamick mill is forgotten with those of Brindle Town, Hanover Furnace, Little Pine Mill, Mount Misery, and Hartshorn—as far as the cutting of lumber is concerned.

That the Hockamick mill survived the others was probably due to the fact that it was small and easy to operate. Its saws and planers persisted in making the woodlands resound even though many of its operators were killed on the scene while at work. Andrew Deal, Daniel Dunfee, Andrew Doron, and John Parker all met sudden and gruesome death on the hexed premises.

Most memorable of the millers of Hockamick were Levi Parker and Big Bill Hartshorn. The last to operate the place

at a profit was John Hutchinson who owned acres of surrounding lands. The mill is falling, piece by piece, as the
years press on, into the water hole below. Inside, old gears
have rusted and under the flooring, the cog wheels are covered with the saffron of old sawdust.

Today the water plunges through a rotting spillway,
flecking with foam the cedar water in the pocket. The
stream was polluted, they say, by sewerage diverted into
the lake in wartime from Camp Dix. Time has glossed over
the resulting controversy and today trout lurk just below
the murky surface, content with Hockamick for a legacy.

There is an old log house beside the town's two dwellings just up the trail from the mill. This was the first house
in Hockamick. It served as a home for woodcutters who
sawed logs at the mill.

There are but two families left of the little group that
once formed a community and gave the town its curious
name. Descendants of those pioneers are in the neighborhood but just where they are and just what they do to live
must remain unknown.

Silence at Hockamick is something that you can feel. It
oppresses you here as it does in other strange villages the
pine country has forgotten. Here once were known the
cries of children, the songs of the woodchopper, the hopes
of honest people cheerful despite their hardships and priva-
tions. Now these are part of the enigma the past has given
the present to solve.

And with the rest, Mick's cough has had its last echo. . . .

Though they who believe in such things will tell you
that he can be heard on a misty night coming up the road
as he did long ago, seeing with cat's eyes, plodding along
with that ugly, harsh, and disturbing "hock."

Swamps like this one at Hog Wallow have long since been planted in cran-

XXXV

HOGLESS HOG WALLOW

Pigs, its has been declared ungrammatically, is pigs. But Hog Wallow has forgotten what a pig looks like. What is more, it is doubtful if Hog Wallow ever saw a wallowing, domesticated pig.

First of all, however, make sure of Hog Wallow's location. Along the road from Chatsworth to the ruins of Harrisia, one passes the settlements Speedwell, Hog Wallow, Pineworth, and Jenkins Neck, in just that order.

Hog Wallow's name harks back to the days when hogs ran wild through the pine barrens. These creatures were probably fugitive from civilized tribes in towns that are forgotten, creatures tired of a primitive civilization, seeking life in the rough.

There are approximately 750,000 acres of barrens in the central portion of Southern New Jersey, blanketed with a sparse growth of pine and oak timber. This pine, known as three-leaf or bull pine, is different from the two-leaf variety of the South. Because of its stunted growth, it has little commercial value.

In this pine country, swamps and lowlands are plentiful. At Hog Wallow the wild hogs found haven, the story goes, wallowing in the muck and cedar water marshes in a neighborhood that was and is well-nigh impassable. Hogs still run wild in the Ozarks but they have vanished from South Jersey; with the advance of time they were hunted for sport and profit and soon became extinct.

The name of the "town," Hog Wallow, stuck, however. To this particular spot came men inclined to invest their capital in cranberries. Where the hogs had wallowed, the swamps were cleared, and were planted in cranberry vines. The work was done by members of the Haines family, who could have chosen a more attractive name for the town, surely, but didn't trouble.

To the uninitiated it would seem that nothing could be done with such land as that which surrounds Hog Wallow. But with money and tools, patience and perseverance, employment has been provided for hundreds of workers and Hog Wallow has yielded pay-berries, blue and cran. There is a large storing and packing house, bleak like the country around it except in season. Then it is a hub of activity, entirely alien to the early days. The plantation is now a part of the operation of Ethelbert Haines, acknowledged authority on lucrative bogs. Land that until a few years ago was assessed as low as twenty-five cents an acre, now has a valuation that has mounted many hundredfold.

Planting a cranberry bog, they told us here, costs about $600 an acre. Planting blueberries costs twice that much. Thousands of dollars have been spent and are being spent in the pines, changing bogs and wallows to land that yields delicacies for tables throughout the world. The pinelands of New Jersey and the Cape Cod country are the nation's cranberry centers.

In connection with the blueberry industry at Hog Wallow, it is interesting to know how the development came about. Elizabeth White, a daughter of Joseph L. White, cranberry king, was chiefly responsible. From the time when she was a child, Miss White accompanied her father on his trips through the bog lands. She soon got the idea that it would be a comparatively simple matter to improve the wild huckleberry.

Miss White offered a substantial money prize to the berry-picker who would locate plants with the choicest fruit. Of these she secured about one hundred and twenty, all but two of which were discarded after a trial growth. From these two, 35,000 hybrid cuttings were made. Of these all but four were later thrown away. From the four a substantial stock has resulted.

The Department of Agriculture gave Miss White its support from the first. Now the New Jersey board is definitely at work in the blueberry industry and about two dozen plantations are increasing their supply. One of these is, of course, at Hog Wallow. The blueberry under cultivation promises to be a delicacy equal to the cranberry, fit for the most discriminating epicurean and of far greater reputation than the wild huckleberry picked by anybody anywhere.

Between Hog Wallow and Speedwell there is a group of buildings, all of different sizes, located in no uniform alignment and in various states of disrepair. Their one uniform feature is the fact that their construction is of the white pine and cedar, frame and shingles, native to the vicinity. This, if you please, is Pineworth, or as its eight or ten natives call it, Worthless City.

There are ruins of several dwellings. There has been a fire, you will see.

"Where's the Post Office?" we asked an unshaven man who was walking casually along the road. We had been told the Post Office would perhaps be one of the sights at Pineworth.

"Burned down," was the reply.

"When?"

"Oh, long ago."

There is no new Post Office, of course. What does a town like this want with a Post Office? Pineworth was on a "star route" and the mail and newspapers came through three times a week.

There used to be a school, too. That was some distance down the road, located in a woods full of rotting piles of discard cranberries. First of all, a school must have pupils, of course, and there weren't enough children in and around Pineworth to maintain a separate school. So the building's empty, weather-beaten and windowless, its walls crudely inscribed by transient wanderers. Schoolchildren of the vicinity now attend classes at a school in Chatsworth, where they are taken in a bus that calls for them along the irregular trail.

The name "Pineworth" came through the original ownership, the owners being George and Jacob Worth. George was a baker and Jacob a butcher. All that was needed was a candlestick-maker. But George and Jake were not the first owners. There had been a man named Messmore.

Messmore, after much litigation over his then apparently worthless holdings, sold out to a chap named McCambridge, who, believe it or not, was the candlestick-maker. Later George Worth sold out his share to Earl Lippincott. Today these men own and control the property. They grow cranberries and enjoy the outdoors.

The location of the new road now is referred to as "near enough." After all, the Pineys like the solitude of their domains. The silence, the mystery, the awesome enigma of the bogs and broken pines may disturb other people, but those who live there are happiest when they are engulfed by all these things. Paved roads, automobiles, surveyors, engineers, people from the cities—all these are intruders.

A tiny chapel at Jenkins Neck was formerly one of the outposts of the Padre of the Pines, an Episcopal missionary who conducted Sunday services in five villages in the Barrens.

The store at Double Trouble, the village that got its name the week muskrats

XXXVI

DOUBLE TROUBLE AND DOVER

When memories of the Rockwell murder near Bamber Lake, venturing beyond the blighted orchards and abandoned station on the Tuckerton line at Cedar Crest, were revived, we made some brief mention of Double Trouble.

Who, we wondered, named it so? Of what depression of the pinelands was such a title a relic? We took the comparatively new concreted Route 40, turning off through Whiting. Then, at the cross-roads where in one direction is beautiful cedar-fringed Bamber Lake and in the other deserted Dover Forge, we took the latter direction.

The road at this point winds and twists through what was once an obvious clearing. In what we had heard of this Cedar Crest in earlier explorations, it was recalled as a fruit town in which the chief product, peaches, failed because of the sandy soil. The hundreds of cleared acres with their dead peach trees tell no story today. Nor do the half dozen shells of houses, left lonely in their midst.

It was at Dover Forge, beyond the sterile orchards, to the east of Ten Mile Hollow, that we heard another version.

Dover Forge was once an important bog ore furnace at almost the geographical center of Ocean County—Monmouth County in those days. Today it is only a cranberry bog. Where the Double Trouble road winds on, a short spur turns to the right among a number of houses.

Before we had come to this turn, however, we had seen

the ruined foundations of several houses along the narrow road, as well as clusters of old and weather-beaten domestic trees. In one clearing was the refuse of a camp and the broken frame of a wooden bed. Then, taking our way along an avenue in which brush and stumps had been cleared, we stumbled on a duck blind along the rushing waters of the Cedar Creek, just in time to frighten several of the fowl into the air. The sudden flapping of their wings gave us all a thrill as they whizzed up and toward us.

From one of the red-roofed shingled buildings at Dover Forge we were greeted by Walter Price and his dog, a terrier that had already sounded an alarm of our approach. Price, caretaker of the bogs for Mrs. Harry Holloway, their present owner, said he had worked, years ago, at Cedar Crest, when the New York Fruit Company established the peach plantation there.

"Of course," said Price, "the borers got those trees in the end, when nobody was left to care for them. But it wasn't the soil that failed them. The peach crop was so big and it ripened so fast one year that the whole output got away from the operators. They couldn't get pickers to work fast enough and the plantation itself, a stock company venture, was too far away to get the peaches to town while they were in condition. If they had had a canning plant on the place, they'd have made a go of it."

Price pointed out the ruined outline of the forge itself, close to the edge of the flooded bog which, at times, is pungent and reddened with cranberries that were left over. To the left of the path that skirts the bog there is a ruined sawmill, its machinery rusted and fallen through the floor.

The cedar water is crystal clear and at the bottom are the well-known relics of slag fragments. Down in the ravine beyond the sawmill are blackened mounds of slag, covered with vines. Here, below the spillway, is a sulphur spring. Price pointed this out as the community refrigerator for all who work at the bog. Jars and crocks are plunged deep in the mineral water which, Price pointed out, is too cold to drink.

"It kills your teeth," he said, "and poisons your gums. But of course nobody here even attempts to drink it."

Price said that the Dover Forge bog was owned by James Applegate, of Toms River, and that Mrs. Holloway is his daughter. Applegate bought a new car some years ago and while in Toms River, cranked it while it was in gear. He was killed.

The Holloways winter in West Creek and summer at Dover Forge. More recently however, Price said, they have been spending more time at the bog because the winters are so pleasant in the pines. Price, who has lived a long time in this section, hasn't thought much about Dover Forge or any of the other lost towns. However, before he returned to sorting moss, gathered in great quantities in the woods for florists in New York City, he told us the way to Double Trouble.

Double Trouble was, in the beginning, a favorite spot of the Indians. They must have had many activities along the Cedar Creek which, with the Jake's Branch of the Toms River, drains this area. Many relics have been found beside the lake itself as well as the many cranberry bogs that have been constructed through the lowlands by the Double Trouble Cranberry Company.

First of all, about that name: According to J. Reed Tilton, superintendent of the bogs whom we found repairing a truck which, because of the wetness of everything thereabouts, had rotted away, said that an old preacher and his wife, and not the Indians, had given the place its peculiar title.

It seems there was once a profusion of muskrats at the end of the lake where, today, the cedar water piles over with such a rush that a foam of white suds tops the surface beyond the sluiceway. The old preacher and those who lived there with him had to repair the dam many times because the wild creatures ate away the barrier. On several occasions, this man, whose name Tilton has forgotten, called out, "Here's trouble!" When the dam was gnawed through twice in one week, the cry became, "Here's double trouble!" And here is Double Trouble to this day—though all that was nearly a hundred years ago.

The Double Trouble Cranberry and Blueberry Company now operates the plantation which includes 3300 acres. The purchase was originally made from the Giberson estate in 1900, but extensions have been made through the cedar lowlands since that time. Just now, the bog planters are more interested in blueberries than cranberries. They are compelled to store away cranberries until they are needed. Blueberries, which are cultivated huckleberries, are increasing in demand.

Double Trouble and Dover Forge lie in a different sort of pinelands than those familiar to travelers nearer the urban areas. There are many hills—mountains, almost, when you recall the barren moors out on the Barnegat Road. There are innumerable ponds and lakes which almost belie their identity with New Jersey. But, nevertheless, here are two towns whose early years have at least survived in newer industries, however foreign they are to iron smelting, cedar logging and fruit growing.

XXXVII

ATSION: ATSAYUNK OF THE ATSIYONKS

IF THERE is anywhere a haunted town, it is Atsion. We had been riding along the bumpy old road that emerges suddenly beside the lake. Our talk had been of ghosts and phantoms, more especially the wraiths of pioneers and memories woven together in frayed legends that lurk behind the doors of these forgotten villages.

Just as we reached the new highway that intrudes upon these fastnesses like a man in dress clothes upon the congregation of a rustic church, it happened.

"I've never been thrilled by ghosts, I don't believe in them," one of us said, flinging the words a little defiantly into the cold sunlight of an early Spring noon.

"Perhaps you will believe in them now."

The words were soft-spoken, a trifle overenunciated. Their effect was such that we looked suddenly, inquiringly, at each other, wondering which one of us had spoken.

At the same time there was a realization that none of US had replied to the measured assertion of disbelief.

"I felt a hand upon my shoulder," I confessed.

All three of us looked in the rumble. Nothing there, that is, nothing that shouldn't have been—boots, rubber coats, a shovel and the rest proved that we had been on these ventures before.

"Balmy," said the man with the camera, with a disdainful shrug toward me. All the same—it was queer.

And so, a little uncertain that just three were in our

269

group, we began to putter around the store, the mansion house and the huge, lopsided old mill of Atsion.

Now that the new road from Bordentown, through Red Lion and skirting old Indian Mills has been finished, automobiles speed in and out of Atsion without knowing it. A few more casual wanderers may wonder, as we did, at the queer name and the things behind it.

Atsion first was Atsayunk, and through this first of names it traces in three syllables its connections with the Indians. It is recorded somewhere that one Lewis Morris, an early settler in "Monmouth Patent," started the first bog iron furnace in New Jersey at Tinton Falls some time prior to 1676. And it is recorded that Joseph Salter, of Toms River, started an iron furnace at Atsayunk in the Mullica River Valley almost 100 years later.

These were days of General John Lacey's Furnace at Ferrago, now Bamber, and also his establishment at New Mills, now Pemberton.

Through these lands there moved a tribe of Indians known as the Mullicas, probably relatives of the Delawares, who took their name from old Eric Mullica, a Swede, who in earlier days had taken up his abode on Little Egg Harbor not far from the present site of Batsto. Still another clan was called the Atsionks, whose principal village was not far from the Atsion of today. Further to the southeast were the Tuckahoes, with whom the Atsionks maintained cordial friendship, both making treks to visit each other and crossing Great Egg Harbor at Innskeep's Ford, below Winslow.

That, you say quickly, was all so long ago. The Red Man, at least, as far as Southern New Jersey is concerned, is forgotten. He and his people may be forgotten, as you say, but continually there are turned up tangible reminders of days before our coming, days when the Indian was lord of all he surveyed.

For instance, out on the old road not far below the little trail swinging in from Indian Mills, is the home of James M. Armstrong. With old recollections of stories that take him and his farmhouse back many years to those of an Indian town, Armstrong, now over seventy, still served his township, Chamong, in the post of tax collector, a trust in which the people retained him thirty years.

It was on this strangely begun first visit to Atsion that we first turned in to see him. He was a little wary, at first, among strangers, and our questions were not as numerous as we made them later. A little uncertain but in no sense feeble, Mr. Armstrong took us to a pipe under one of his barns, stamped with the letter "A."

"That came from Atsion's furnace," he said.

We told him that at Atsion they said he held the keys to all the old stories of Atsion. He only smiled. He said he had lived in the same house sixty-seven years and ought to know the country "fairly good." There were others in the house; we seemed to be intruding, and so pressed on.

Atsion is chiefly distinguished by a new bridge, constructed by the State, and damming the lake, for the first time with certainty. A new span was built not very long ago, but it had to be pulled apart. Below the spillway, a series of sluices, we found the ruined fragments of walls that were once part of the furnace layout.

Behind this, across a wide clearing to the tall mill structure, one can trace the numerous excavations made for bog ore. The meandering, sluggish Atsion Creek winds on toward Hampton Gate. The ground is carpeted with slag,

bits of old brick and larger lumps of refuse from the forge.
Behind the mill, across an impassable marsh of stagnant
water, once the rushing stream that turned the great wheels,
there is one huge mass that years ago was molten. Upon
its crest a large pine snake lay befuddled in the sun.

We turned back toward the house, a mansion with large
porticos all but surrounding its yellow walls. The pillars
we found to be iron, embossed at the base with the familiar
"A." The woodwork was soggy. Turning from the box-
wood, two of us ran up on the porch.

The shutters were closed. There was a promise of shade
from the gnarled old buttonwoods, not yet in leaf. From
the dam, yet under construction at that time, came the staccato clatter of a mechanical device. We knocked on the
huge old door.

If this were court, I would, perhaps, think twice about
it. But I do swear here to hearing footsteps inside and a
faint tinkering with a bolt on the other side of the barrier.
The door itself did not move. It did not swing open.

Wondering if something had happened to the man who
had answered the knock and then seemed to have decided
differently, I gingerly touched the bottom with my foot.
The door suddenly swung wide. There was no one in the
hall.

"Hello," we called, surprise providing gooseflesh. There
was an echo worthy of the best ghost stories. From the hallway came a musty smell, that of bran and damp grain. We
walked in. The place was gloomy. The front rooms, high-
ceilinged, were filled with rude bins. The floor over which
dancers once gracefully swept, was littered with chicken
feed and dried corn.

Of course, it was noon. The storekeeper, whose place was next door, was, we decided afterward, undoubtedly chuckling over his dinner while we used our imaginations too freely.

But there WAS something behind that door—call it a marauding rat, if you will.

This was the Richards' mansion. On our second call at Mr. Armstrong's farm we heard his story of it as his two grandchildren, wide-eyed, lingered listening to the tale. The house was the center of what social life there was in the days of Samuel, Jesse and William Richards. There was originally 56,000 acres in the Atsion tract. Bog ore was mined, charcoal was made and lumbering was a paying business.

The elder Richards divided his holdings at Atsion between a son and daughter. These rights included operations then at Martha, Hampton, Speedwell and even old Weymouth. The ninety-odd thousand acres in the Weymouth tract were parcelled out to two other children.

Young William Richards and his sister, Maria, inherited the Atsion property. Maria married a Belgian named Fleming, according to Mr. Armstrong's recollections, and this fellow was soon mixed up in legal complications. Fleming quickly departed with his wife and did not return. William, however, continued to live on the old road over which we came, the way to Dellett.

Fleming had made an assignment of his wife's holdings to Colonel William Patterson, of Philadelphia, a brother of the General, Robert Patterson, who figured prominently in the Battle of Bull Run. Jesse Richards, born December 2, 1772, died, according to the inscription on his tombstone, at Pleasant Mills, June 17, 1854. Colonel Patterson came to Atsion in 1862, after the beginning of the Civil War, but he soon sold his share to Morris Rawley.

Fleming had tried to manufacture paper in the old furnace buildings without success. Rawley, with as much courage, sought to make the place a cotton milling center. It was he who enlarged the largest of the present buildings to three stories, adding four times as much of the structure as was originally there. Yarn was turned out for some years.

These were days of railroad romances, trickery of rivals to put down tracks that were to open up new land and feed new industrial enterprises. According to Armstrong, the first railroad (not the present route of the Jersey Central) reached Atsion in 1863. The Camden-Amboy Company, which held control of the railroads hereabouts, sought to head off all competition to its Philadelphia-New York line.

The Delaware & Raritan Bay Company, however, won the right to put down a track to Atco. From this, through a trick hidden in a charter's phrasing, a spur line was put down from Atco to Atsion. There are many who do not even now know of the existence of this single-track line, which, at the beginning, was part of a route to New York.

The spur is there, at least part of it, today, one section being used as a street in Atco. Back of Atsion there is another section, its rails rusted and ties sagging, overgrown with tall weeds. Unused and unexplained, it passes by an old cemetery which is altogether forgotten by those who think of the little burial ground behind the Atsion chapel as Atsion's official plot. Graves are caving in and most of the stones have toppled over.

On one is inscribed "John Ross, son of John and Dolly

The old stove in the Crosswicks Meeting was made at Atsion, one of four pre-Revolutionary forges started by Charles Read, friend of Benjamin Franklin and holder of many public offices.

The site of Hampton Furnace far up the Batsto River.

The old stage road to Eagle, once noted for its hotel.

Ross, of the Parish of Madgiligan, Ireland, who departed this life Feb. 22, 1804, Aged 20 years." On another is "Robert McNeill, Died May 6, 1865, Aged 55 years." These were probably pioneers of the Roman Catholic group which was strong at Batsto and with the help of the elder Richards once reared a church. Here, forgotten with the railroad line which served early and more prosperous days, they sleep under the pines on the lake shore.

"Nothing much has been done at Atsion, since Rawley died," Mr. Armstrong said. "Of course, you saw the Etheridge store." This building, a quaint little affair with something like a belfry at the top, looked more like a church. Up at the point of its roof we remembered the date, 1827.

"Was there ever a monastery at Atsion?" we asked the Township collector bluntly, as we had planned to. The legend had been following us about for a long time.

"No," Armstrong said, with emphatic certainty. They had told us, we said, that the main building was used by the priests and that the store had been their chapel. We heard such a story from no less a person than Mayor Clifford String, of Oaklyn, who likes to browse around old Atsion.

"You can see that never was a church," Armstrong said. "Those two doors at the front, upstairs and downstairs, show it was always what it is now—just a store."

"What about the bell in its belfry?"

I got up quickly. I half suspected that photographers can be ventriloquists if they choose. But this one was as startled as I. It was the same kind of voice that had spoken from behind the car on that first day. I looked at the old farmer. He had heard nothing, evidently.

As if I had to do it or choke on the words, I repeated the question, that none of US had asked:

"What about the bell in the belfry?"

Armstrong did not think there was a bell concealed there. He doesn't know, but he said he never heard of one.

The Atsion property is now part of that vast tract owned by the heirs of the Wharton Estate who seek to make it a great water source for New Jersey. It was Colonel Wharton who planted many strange trees through the domain. Scotch firs up the Dellett Road are dying with a kind of blight. Other evergreens stand near by in formation.

The Atsion seer suddenly went into the house and when he emerged he held in his hand a box, full and running over with those reminders of the Indians. In his years on the farm—sixty-seven of them—Armstrong has filled that box with 118 pieces, as the systematic inscription will tell you, arrowheads, spear-points, skin-scrapers. There are various types of stone, and that, our friend pointed out, testified either to the warlike activities of the Atsyonks or Edge-Pollocks.

Armstrong said that Dr. Charles Philhower, of Westfield, who was down to see his relics not so long ago, preferred to believe that the bits of Indian weapons traced great sociability and movement of the tribes. One particular piece of stone, Dr. Philhower pointed out, must have come from Lake Cayuga.

The Richards burial plot, where much of the history of the old town is told, is beside the church at Pleasant Mills. Here lie the Richards—Elizabeth, who became Mrs. Thomas Haskins, wife of the Rev. Thomas Haskins, Abbigail Sarah Knox, the Moores and the Kenneys.

Funerals from Atsion to Pleasant Mills must have been picturesque. The connecting trail winds through the woods, burned black by the devastating fires of Spring. As we made the journey, much more quickly by modern means, deer leaped from drinking places along the upper lake, rabbits scurried for shelter in the brambles, crows cawed, buzzards soared dismally overhead. Picture a funeral of yesteryear passing slowly all day across this tortuous path, through wild woodlands such as these, and you have a cross-section of life and death as Atsion knew them.

Shamong Township's first white citizen was Micajah Willetts, who prior to the Revolutionary War located near Indian Mills. The Willettses, the Joneses, Pricketts, Masons all have been linked with Atsion since the first. Here, with the site of the Indian reservation at Indian Mills included, was one of John Brainerd's missionary fields. The tiny white chapel on the hill carries on his work.

There are a few weather-beaten, unpainted houses up the chapel road. Near the railroad station is another group, their roofs aslant as if they were discussing what is to become of their town.

In the hope of some new strange manifestation to complete those queer happenings at Atsayunk of the Atsiyonks, we made one more, a sort of final visit. The sun was blazing down on the blinding sand-rims of the new road. There was no breeze to whisper in the pines. Beside the lake shore whose waters hide snags of stumps, campers from the city had pitched their tents.

On strings before them were bathing suits, shirts, flimsy wearing apparel. Parked among the trees were weather-stained automobiles. The smell of gasoline filled the grove.

New gravel on the old trail threw up a smoke-screen behind a speeding car. One tree was bleeding from a purposeless ax-wound. A swimmer was bubbling loudly the cedar water.

We returned home. The least self-respecting ghost, be he from the unkempt graveyard or the cupola that may be a belfry, has no further business in this new Atsion.

THE END

A NOTE ON THE AUTHOR

HE was a concert violinist, an author, an Episcopal priest. He taught in a one-room school, labored as a young Camden newspaperman, won state-wide fame as a folklorist. He led tours in the Pine Barrens and lectured everywhere. He was the first to write extensively about the state, and he wrote with such warmth and enthusiasm that at least two generations of people who believe in New Jersey fell under his spell and owe an enduring debt to him. Despite his accomplishments, he never became pompously serious. He was Henry Charlton Beck.

Two careers beckoned to him after graduation from Haddonfield High School: the ministry and music. He enrolled at Virginia Theological Seminary after high school but never attended because of lack of money. He played in concert orchestras for fifteen years, but he never made it to the big time of music. Extremely bright, but without formal qualifications, he taught in a one-room school immediately after leaving high school.

When Henry Beck was twenty, he joined the Camden *Courier-Post* as a cub reporter. He saw his typewriter as an instrument of expression; shortly before his death he defined his career: "I just sit down and tap it out like any rewriteman." The "tapping" turned out six detective novels, all published but none distinguished. Assigned to write about South Jersey in the early 1930s, the young newspaperman found himself enthralled by tales spun to him in Penny Pot, Apple Pie Hill, and Ong's Hat, in Batsto, Calico, and Crowleytown. He had found his life. He listened, he tapped out his stories, and he became known to a limited *Courier-Post* readership.

Then, in 1936, E. P. Dutton gathered together his early newspaper stories and published them as *Forgotten Towns of Southern New Jersey.*

It was a smash hit. Other books followed on New Jersey, six in all. His knowledge of the state made him the logical choice to be editor of Rutgers University Press for a brief tenure (1945–1947). His emphasis on folklore led to the founding of the New Jersey Folklore Society, with Henry C. Beck the only possible choice for president.

His desire to be a minister never waned. He studied for the Episcopal priesthood while at Rutgers Press and received ordination in 1949. He preached and he ministered, and did so very well, yet he continued writing a weekly full-page article for the Newark *Star-Ledger.*

A listing of his accomplishments, however distinguished, does Henry Beck only slight credit. It tells little of this gentle, witty man except that he worked far beyond the capacity of most of us. It tells nothing of his charm as a guide through the Pine Barrens, nothing of his kindnesses to the few of us who were just beginning as writers when he was at his peak.

He was often called a historian but he insisted that he was "only a folklorist." His goal was to seek out those who have lived history, have them tell it in their own terms. He was, in fact, an oral historian long before the National Endowment for the Humanities poured out funds to make oral history academically respectable. Because of his books, Father Beck may be regarded by some as a historian. But his leg often was pulled by those whom he interviewed, and he, in turn, could put entertainment above scholarship. Above all, be sure of this: he never wittingly gave less than his best.

Henry C. Beck died in 1965. Those of us who knew his varied, parallel careers and who encountered his name from High Point to Cape May were surprised to learn that he was only sixty-two years old when he died. Few persons accomplish so much in so short a time.